ROSE FROM
BRIER

ROSE FROM BRIER

BY

AMY CARMICHAEL

DOHNAVUR FELLOWSHIP

TO

MARY

WHO BESTOWED MUCH LABOR ON ME

CHRISTIAN LITERATURE CRUSADE
Fort Washington, Pennsylvania 19034

CHRISTIAN LITERATURE CRUSADE

U.S.A.
P.O. Box 1449, Fort Washington, PA 19034

GREAT BRITAIN
51 The Dean, Alresford, Hants., SO24 9BJ

AUSTRALIA
P.O. Box 91, Pennant Hills, N.S.W. 2120

NEW ZEALAND
10 MacArthur Street, Feilding

ISBN 0-87508-077-4

Copyright 1933
The Dohnavur Fellowship

First published 1933
First American Edition 1971

This edition 1973
This printing 1996
by permission of
The Dohnavur Fellowship

PRINTED IN THE UNITED STATES OF AMERICA

ROSE FROM BRIER

"From thy brier shall blow a rose for others."

Letters written originally to the Dohnavur Fellowship Invalids' League, but now shared with any ill who care to have this rose from our brier.

And I heard a great voice out of heaven saying, Behold, the tabernacle of God is with men, and He will dwell with them, and they shall be His people, and God Himself shall be with them, and be their God.

And God shall wipe away all tears from their eyes; and there shall be no more death, neither sorrow nor crying, neither shall there be any more pain: for the former things are passed away.

LIST OF ILLUSTRATIONS

TO THE TRUE NURSE

GOD'S own true nurse is she who knows
   "By constant watching wise"
Just where the scalding current flows
   That, hid from casual eyes,
Makes life an arid wilderness;
Then does the true nurse bless.

For she, without the noise of words
   Most lovingly will do,
Till, like the song of happy birds,
   The joy of ease pours through
That which was arid wilderness—
So does the true nurse bless.

And when the spirit drifts afraid
   To strange and unknown lands,
Then does the true nurse, undismayed
   (Her dear love understands),
Follow and comfort and caress—
So does the true nurse bless.

O nurse, God-given, your ministry
   Is something all divine;
With all you do, in all you be,
   His love will intertwine
The gold threads of His gentleness—
So will His true nurse bless.

THE ROSE

PROPERLY speaking, this is not a book at all, but only a bundle of letters. They were written in pencil a little at a time; they could not have felt formal if they had tried.

But by the time such fragments are laboriously typed (by faithful Lotus Buds), and printed, bound, and given a name, they look like a book, and reading them through I am troubled to find them so personal and sometimes so intimate. It is not that I think the personal or the intimate interesting or valuable, but that I did not know how to give the comfort wherewith we ourselves are comforted without giving something of my own soul also. If I had waited till the harrow had lifted, perhaps a less tired mind would have found a better way. But then the book would have been from the *well* to the ill, and not from the *ill* to the ill, which I think is what it is meant to be—a rose plucked straight from a brier.

There is no ordered sequence in the letters. There is no ordered sequence in the way the trials and temptations and the weary little feelings of illness fling themselves upon us, hurling their forces ruthlessly upon an already weakened front. But with

9

them, anticipating them rather, there is always the succor of the very present Help.

All these letters have been written, as one of them tells, what time the storm fell upon me, not after the coming of the calm. In the *Meditations* of Marcus Aurelius we are told that it is in our power to live free from all compulsion in the greatest tranquillity of mind, even if wild beasts tear in pieces the members of this kneaded matter which has grown around us. "For what hinders the mind, in the midst of all this, from maintaining itself in tranquillity?" But when he wrote that, his kneaded matter was not being torn in pieces. It was sitting comfortably aloof from the claws of wild beasts; so his composure does not do much for us. It can, indeed, be exceedingly irritating. There is more of the pith of life in Satan's "Put forth Thine hand now and touch his bone and his flesh"— we understand that.

> The toad beneath the harrow knows
> Exactly where each tooth-point goes;
> The butterfly upon the road
> Preaches contentment to that toad.

There can be minutes when the toad is not properly grateful to the butterfly—no, not even if he comes dressed like a very good Christian. He is upon the road: he isn't under the harrow; he never was there.

Such a minute came one morning when all I wanted was something which would help me to escape from myself; and there is nothing that can so quickly give this release as a book that takes me out of my own life into the lives of others.

Just then the post came—"And a book packet!" said my dear nurse. Her voice with its note of expectation was as delightful as what we hoped would be the contents of that parcel. Eagerly she opened it and eagerly I watched her. Would it be something like Bernard Allen's *Gordon and the Sudan*, which I had just read, or John Buchan's latest story? (No writer could carry me off to the heather just then as he could.) But no—that fat parcel was full of tracts for the sick. I tried those tracts, but somehow they took me nowhere. This sounds most unmissionary; unhappily, it is true. It was not till some time later, and after several similar experiences, that it struck me perhaps the reason was because they were obviously written by the well to the ill, to do them good; and so they could only flutter past like ineffective butterflies. But I found that things written by those who were in pain themselves, or who had passed through pain to peace, like the touch of understanding in a dear human letter, did something that nothing except the words of our eternal Lord could ever do.

So these letters purposely go forth from under the harrow before the sharpness of the prod of a single tooth is forgotten. They go to some who are under far sharper harrows, and they carry all they can to them of sympathy that understands. They are not, of course, meant to be read straight through; that would be intolerably tedious. Nor will every letter fit every mood. Illness has its moods. But I hope that they will not irritate any poor toad.

And now, in the twenty-second month of this new

way of living—the way that began with "Your joy"—the proofs of these letters have come; and with a greater diffidence than ever I let them go. They go to some who are disappointed. They hoped to be well long ago and are not well yet. This little song is for them, and then for the others, never forgotten, for whom the end of illness will be heaven:

Before the winds that blow do cease,
   Teach me to dwell within Thy calm:
Before the pain has passed in peace,
   Give me, my God, to sing a psalm.
Let me not lose the chance to prove
   The fullness of enabling love.
O Love of God, do this for me:
   Maintain a constant victory.

Before I leave the desert land
   For meadows of immortal flowers,
Lead me where streams at Thy command
   Flow by the borders of the hours,
That when the thirsty come, I may
   Show them the fountains in the way.
O Love of God, do this for me:
   Maintain a constant victory.

THE PHOTOGRAPHS

THEY are the work of Dr. Defner of Innsbruck ("the harvest of a quiet eye").

It was a kind chance that brought these pictures to us. We have for our blessing one at home who is always on the lookout for little, happy, unexpected things in London shops. And she sent us the water lily (water-rose it calls itself in its own country). It happened to come on a day, all ill people know such days, when everything was heavy to hold, and the little card was just what I wanted. Then I thought of the ill everywhere and wished that they could have it too. Would it not rest them, I thought within myself, just to look at the cool water and the pure flower ("something between a thought and a thing"), so still and so content? They would find a tiny separate joy in each tiny separate detail, the crystal drop on the petal, the reflection, the dim stems under water, even the triangular tear in the leaf; a water lily leaf, like a lotus leaf, seems always to tear in that way.

Then came the horse chestnut in spring; and now I could use a large magnifying-glass, and seen so, the leafiness and the candle-flowers carried me out into green woods miles away from any "sick-room." And the desire came to give *Rose from Brier* these dear things. So one of us wrote to Dr. Defner, who replied delightfully, "It was a special joy to me to hear that my works, which of course must be kept within the discreet limits of photography, have reached even far-away India and found kind judgment there." And the end of the story is, these four pictures, the gift of four of us to you, our friends, who are ill. (Our doctor gives the snowdrop, our nurse-in-chief the water lily.) There are no words printed underneath. I leave each reader to fit them into their own places in the letters. The water lily will find its word for some on one page, for some on another. To me it belongs to the letter beginning

> "As John upon his dear Lord's breast,
> "So would I lean, so would I rest."

May its peacefulness carry consolation to some tired heart. May the glory of the chestnuts speak not of a vanished spring, but of that to which we are hastening; may the snowdrops remind someone oppressed by the things that are seen, of the things that shall be seen, the Father's heavenly surprises (what flowers of eternal wonder are folded in the coverlet of snow?). And may the Hand that was pierced by more than thorns of brier touch and bless this little book, and cause briers to bloom with roses wherever it goes—roses that will never fade away.

CONTENTS

IF thou walk inwardly, thou shalt not weigh flying words. . . . Let not thy peace be in the mouths of men.

Certainly, Thou being present, all things are jocund, and Thou being absent, all things are loth and weary. Thou makest in the heart tranquillity, great peace, and solemn gladness. Thou makest man to feel well of all, and in all things to praise Thee, nor there may no thing long please without Thee; but, if it shall be acceptable and savour well, it behoveth Thy grace to be nigh and to make it savoury with the sauce of Thy wisdom. To whom Thou savourest, what shall not savour to him aright? And to whom Thou savourest not, what thing may turn him to mirth?

The Imitation
(From MS. in the University
Library at Cambridge).

So you will ride at ease over the breakers of this mortal life and not care too much what befalls you —not from carelessness, but from the soaring gladness of heavenly love.

Life and Letters of Janet Erskine Stuart,
by Maud Monahan.

1. YOUR JOY

A STRANGE first word, but it was the first that came to me, so it begins the story of these happy months.

For they have been happy: I say this to myself with wonder, for, indeed, it is very wonderful to me that it can be true, even though such love has been round about me, and so many helps have been given, that it would be difficult as well as ungrateful to be unhappy. But I cannot help wondering over it, for to be with my family all day and every day was life to me, and nothing could keep me in bed, not even illness; at worst I made a deck-chair serve. I never thought of being tied to bed all day long. I had expected to be strengthened to ignore or tread under foot bodily ills, and (having earnestly asked for this) to pass on straight from the midst of things without giving anyone any trouble. What had happened, then, was strange to me; "And the Lord hath hid it from me, and hath not told me," was my puzzled inward attitude. So the shining happiness, through months when will-power could do nothing to conquer pain (and it could not be ignored), was not natural, but one of those surprises of our heavenly Lover, who never seems to tire of giving us surprises.

The first word that came was unsought. It was the morning after the accident (which, briefly, was a fall in the little town of Joyous City, where some of us had gone to prepare for the two who were to live there. This fall broke a bone, dislocated an ankle, and caused other hurts much harder to heal). I had been taken to Neyyoor, in Travancore, a drive of forty-six miles from Joyous City, and the effects of the merciful morphia were beginning to wear off, when I heard someone say something about wishing to take the pain from me. It was our nurse-in-chief, Mary Mills, who had stayed after our doctor, May Powell, and the others had returned to Dohnavur; and I knew she meant that she wanted to bear it herself instead of me. Then I heard myself answer, *Your joy no man taketh from you.* It was like echoing aloud something heard deep within me. I did not recognize it as a text, but just as a certain and heavenly word given to me for whoever should want to do that loving thing.

It was truly a word of peace, even of exultation. I could see our whole great family, and each one old enough to understand, wanting to do that same thing. I was glad and grateful that it was impossible.

And now, that I may show why I do humbly feel I can venture to write to those who know so much more of the awful trampling power of pain than I do, I will tell how it was that the thought came to write.

One day, after weeks of nights when, in spite of all that was done to induce sleep, it refused to come, except in brief distracted snatches, the mail brought a letter which discoursed with what sounded almost like pleasure on this "enforced rest," and the silly phrase rankled like a thorn. I was far too tired to laugh it off as one can laugh off things when one is well. So *this* was supposed to be rest? and was the Father breaking, crushing, "forcing," by weight of sheer physical misery, a child who only longed to obey His lightest wish? This word had what I now know was an absurd power to distress. It held such an unkind, such a false conception of our Father. Till that hour, although I was puzzled, I had not had one unhappy minute. I had been given peace in acceptance. The spirit can live above the flesh, and mine, helped by the tender love of our Lord Jesus and the dearness of all around me, had done so.

But in that hour it was different, and I had no peace till I had heard deep within me soft and soothing words such as a mother uses: "Let not your heart be troubled; do I not understand? What do such words matter to Me or to thee?" And I knew that the Father understood His child, and the child her Father, and all was peace again.

Then, like the scent of a flower blown by a passing wind, came the memory of a day in the train some years ago. I was travelling to Puri, a thousand miles north of Dohnavur, on the Father's business, when a silly feather-flutter of local gossip, retailed by a guest before she could be stopped, tried to disturb me. And it did disturb till these six words were repeated over and over, beaten out, as it were, in my ear by the sound of the wheels of the train: "Let it be; think of Me." These words spoke to me again now.

It was then that the thought of the many to whom unrecorded little pangs must be daily commonplaces came with a new compassion, born of a new understanding. And I wanted to share my crumb of comfort at once, and tell them not to weigh flying words, or let their peace be in the mouths of men, or allow the ignorant stock phrases of the well to the ill to penetrate their shield. "For no man can tell what in that combat attends us but he that hath been in the battle himself "; so how can they, the unwounded, know anything about the matter? But the Lord our Creator knows (and all who have ever suffered know) that pain and helplessness are not rest, and never can be; nor is the weakness that follows acute pain, nor the tiredness that is so tired of being tired that it is poles apart from rest. He knows that rest is found in that sense of well-being one has after a gallop on horseback, or a plunge in a forest pool or the glorious sea—in physical and in mental fitness, in power to be and do. He knows it. He created us so, and does the Creator forget? If He remembers, what does it matter that others forget? Thus, being comforted and filled with inward sweetness, we can thank Him for all who trample unawares upon us, talking smooth nothings. For we know, just because they can do it so unconsciously, so easily, and with so airy a grace, that they, at least, were never laid in iron; and is *that* not good to know?

MOST FINE GOLD

I THOUGHT I heard my Saviour say to me,
"My love will never weary, child, of thee."
Then in me, whispering doubtfully and low,
  "How can that be?"
  He answered me,
"But if it were not so,
I would have told thee."

> *O most fine Gold*
> *That nought in me can dim,*
> *Eternal Love, that has her home in Him*
> *Whom, seeing not, I love,*
> *I worship Thee.*

I thought I heard my Saviour say to me,
"My strength encamps on weakness—so on thee";
And when a wind of fear did through me blow,
  "How can that be?"
  He answered me,
"But if it were not so
I would have told thee."

> *O most fine Gold*
> *That nought in me can dim,*
> *Eternal Love, that has her home in Him*
> *Whom, seeing not, I love,*
> *I worship Thee.*

2. HIS SOUL ENTERED INTO IRON

Now that I have told why I am venturing to write at all, I will tell how words of peace and deliverance began to come, words that seemed to make the impossible possible; and to tell this in order means to go back to the beginning.

It was Sunday evening, October 25, 1931. Dr. Somervell and Dr. Orr of Neyyoor, instead of enjoying a Sunday evening off after their crowded week, took me down from Dr. Somervell's bungalow to the X-ray room in the L.M.S. Hospital, where Dr. Orr gave the anesthetic. Just before he began to do so, Dr. Somervell prayed that the ankle might be "made strong to bear burdens again," and the next thing of which I was aware was a lovely wakening with these words in my ear, "My times are in Thy hand." Before the foot was touched I had asked Dr. Somervell how long it would be till I could get back to work, and he had said that it must be in splints for eight weeks. I had taken this to mean that all would be well in eight weeks. It had seemed like eight years to look forward to. I never dreamt of what really lay ahead, but here I was awakening with the right word for whatever it was to be—"My times," those eight weeks as it seemed then, "are in Thy hand," and the next line of the old familiar hymn followed of itself, "My God, I wish them there."

For some days the pain was dulled; then it came on with a severity which was to increase for many weeks (and, in one form or another, months), and the day that opened into this new experience found me with a heretofore not much noticed word from Psalm 105: 18 in our A.V., "Whose feet they hurt with fetters; he was laid in iron," but in the LXX*, "His soul entered into iron." A footnote in Kay's translation explains it: his soul "entered," whole and entire, in its resolve to obey God, into the cruel torture. My soul was not in cruel torture, but my foot was hurt with fetters, and as I lay, unable to move, it came to me that what was asked of Joseph in a far greater degree was asked of me now. Would I just "thole it," and pray for grace not to make too much of it, or would my soul enter willingly into the iron of this new experience?

There could be only one answer to that. And when on the following Sunday evening a word was given from Philippians 1:13, "My bonds in Christ," I knew that all was well indeed.

And a poem came my way, too, just then (for we were in one of those dear homes of the earth where little children, and books, and an abounding loving-kindness ease illness at every turn). It was Evelyn Underhill's *Stigmata*, of which one verse spoke with a special tenderness:

*Septuagint

Must I be wounded in the untiring feet
That hasted all the way
My Dear to greet?
Shall errant love endure this hard delay,
Limping and slow
On its ascents to go?

> *Yea, this must be*
> *If thou wouldst come with Me:*
> *Thus only can*
> *My seal be set on man.*

So there could be nothing but a peaceful acceptance, and when one accepts, all that is included in the thing accepted is accepted too—the helplessness, the limitations, the disappointments of hope deferred, the suffering.

I think this must be important to the clearness of our spiritual atmosphere, for if we let the fugitive wisp of a cloud, which we call a wish (a wish that things were different), float across our sky, then swiftly the whole sweet blue is overcast. But if we refuse that wisp of cloud and look up and meet the love of the Lord that shines down on us, and say to Him about that particular detail of trial, "Dear Lord, yes" (for was it not included in the first act of acceptance?) then in one bright moment our sky is blue again.

HE opened the rock, and the waters gushed out; they ran in the dry places like a river (Ps. 105:41).

For the Lord shall comfort Zion: He will comfort all her waste places; and He will make her wilderness like Eden, and her desert like the garden of the Lord; joy and gladness shall be found therein, thanksgiving, and the voice of melody (Isa. 51:3).

> In the shadow of His wings
> I will sing for joy;
> What a God, who out of shade
> Nest for singing bird hath made;
> *Lord, my Might and Melody,*
> *I will sing to Thee.*

> If the shadow of Thy wings
> Be so full of song,
> What must be the lighted place
> Where Thy bird can see Thy face?
> *Lord, my Might and Melody,*
> *I will sing to Thee.*

3. ALL HIS COUCH HAST THOU TRANS-FORMED

PEACE in acceptance: to my reading of the Scriptures, pain (like sin and cruelty) is the work of the enemy—"An enemy hath done this." If it were not so we should, I think, have no right to resist it. We do not resist our Lord; if it be His dear hand that "presseth sore," as one of His saints wrote, then we could not and should not push it off, or try to slip from under it. All the wonderful easers of pain, which I believe are His gift, would be forbidden to us. Doctors and nurses would not be working with Him, but against Him. We hold to His words, "Ought not this woman whom Satan hath bound, lo, these eighteen years, to be loosed from this bond?" leaving the mystery behind them (so often present with us) for Him to explain in His time.

As I lay for two hours or more in the dark on the sand at Joyous City before help came, that which had to be endured seemed to give a sharpness to thought. I thought of men tormented, not by accident, but on purpose, in this same town and many another Eastern town. I stood alongside the English judge who at that time openly fought torture in this district. I blessed

God afresh for every man, whosoever he be, who fights that infernal thing in this or any land. And as one may look through a very small window upon a very great view, I saw in a new way a fragment of what we mean when we say *Calvary* (but I will write of that again). The ministry of doctors and nurses appeared to me more than ever before as a divine thing then, and I felt that our Lord Jesus, beholding them, must love them, and greatly desire to work together with them, laying His hand upon theirs as they work, in guidance and benediction.

So though through these months *acceptance* has been a word of liberty and victory and peace to me, it has never meant acquiescence in illness, as though ill-health were from Him who delights to deck His priests with health. But it did mean contentment with the unexplained. Neither Job nor Paul ever knew (so far as we know) why prayer for relief was answered as it was. But I think that they must stand in awe and joy, as they meet others in the heavenly country who were strengthened and comforted by their patience and valor, and the record of their Father's thoughts of peace toward them. Hardly a life that goes deep but has tragedy somewhere within it; what would such do without Job? And who could spare from his soul's hidden history the great words spoken to St. Paul,. "My grace is sufficient for thee, for My strength is made perfect in weakness"? Such words lead straight to a land where there is gold, and the gold of that land is good.

Gold—the word recalls Job's affirmation, "When He hath tried me I shall come forth as gold"; and St.

Peter's "The trial of your faith, being much more precious than of gold that perisheth, though it be tried with fire"; and the quiet word in Malachi, "He shall sit as a refiner and purifier of silver." I have often thanked God that the word is not gold there, but silver. Silver is of little account in the East, and we feel more like silver than gold. But He shall sit as a refiner and purifier of *silver,* so who need fear?

This picture of the Refiner is straight from Eastern life. The Eastern goldsmith sits on the floor by his crucible. For me, at least, it was not hard to know why the Heavenly Refiner had to sit so long. The heart knows its own dross. Blessed be the love that never wearies, never gives up hope that even in such poor metal He may at last see the reflection of His face. "How do you know when it is purified?" we asked our village goldsmith. "When I can see my face in it," he answered.

I was wondering one day how such happiness as this that He was giving could possibly be, when everything that was happening was so objectionable, so detestable to the natural man. I knew, of course, that it was nothing in me that caused it to be. Was it because of the love of my dearest that lapped me in soft waves all round? But even that could not account for it (though, indeed, He only knows how very much it helped), for I had heard of it in far more alien air, in rooms where there was no love, and keener, more prolonged suffering. Our Invalids' League supplied such miracles. What accounted for them?

That day I was reading in the Psalms, as translated

by Rotherham, and came upon Psalm 41:3, *All his couch hast Thou transformed in his disease*—a transformed bed, word of peace and wonder. Sustained upon the bed of sickness: "The Lord comfort him when he lieth sick upon his bed"; "Make Thou all his bed in his sickness"—each rendering adds a small, new, tender note—"The Lord will strengthen him upon the bed of languishing" (true name for bed as it can be at times); "Do Thou so make my bed in all my sickness" (this was Donne's prayer) "that being used to Thy hand, I may be content with any bed of Thy making."

Does not this account for the happiness of those who, like His great missionary prisoner St. Paul, have very little or nothing of human help to make a cheer? An unkind word, a careless touch (trials never once mine), cannot shatter a happiness that has its source in the hills of God. "They shall be satisfied with the plenteousness of Thy house, and Thou shalt give them drink of Thy pleasures, as out of the river," is the Prayer-Book version of Psalm 36:8, and Rotherham's "Out of the full stream of Thine own pleasures Thou givest them to drink," has a footnote: "more literally, *torrent*." But to understand that word as used by an Eastern writer one should have seen a mountain torrent after rain. There is such a magnificent abandon about it, such a sense of force that no power on earth can fetter, that one gazes in awe and in wonder. Words cannot capture the sense of that glorious conquering fullness of might. You watch the floods of white foaming waters rushing down: they appear to be eternal, filled from some exhaustless reservoir in the heights.

O Lord of the waters that run in our dry places like a river, O Comforter of all our waste places, dear Lord of the still waters too, we drink, and we are satisfied.

FOR us swords drawn, up to the gates of heaven,
Oh may no coward spirit seek to leaven
The warrior code, the calling that is ours;
Forbid that we should sheathe our sword in flowers.

Swords drawn,
Swords drawn,
Up to the gates of heaven—
For us swords drawn
Up to the gates of heaven.

Captain belovèd, battle wounds were Thine,
Let me not wonder if some hurt be mine;
Rather, O Lord, let my deep wonder be
That I may share a battle-wound with Thee.

O golden joy that Thou, Lord, givest them
Who follow Thee to far Jerusalem;
O joy immortal, when the trumpets sound,
And all the world is hushed to see Thee crowned

4. SWORDS DRAWN

I HAVE told how the stock phrase about "enforced rest" rankled on a day when half of my kneaded matter was held fast in iron, and the other half lay in a lassitude that was very far from rest. Another of those flying words addressed to the sick came in letters occasionally; it was about being "laid aside." It was the sort of thing one might say to a cracked china cup: "Poor dear, you are laid aside." But then the Lord's servant is not a china cup. He (she) is a soldier. Soldiers may be wounded in battle and sent to hospital. A hospital isn't a shelf; it is a place of repair. And a soldier on service in the spiritual army is never off his battlefield. He is only removed to another part of the field when a wound interrupts what he meant to do, and sets him doing something else.

So when a letter came from one who was about to join our Fellowship, quoting from his fiancée's letter to him, "I know that for us it is to be swords drawn, up to the gates of heaven," I found great delight in the word. The song that came out of those words was written without a thought of my own minute and passing battle wound. I was thinking of the so much greater and more protracted trials that might be part of life for these two—for married life, if both husband and wife are pledged soldiers, is a sacrificial thing from the first day. But now that the song is sung to its kindling music I have sometimes let it turn to present comfort. And I would pass it on to all hurt soldiers everywhere. Is it not joy, pure joy, that there is no question of the shelf?

No soldier on service is ever "laid aside"; he is only given another commission, sometimes just to suffer (we are not told yet the use of that), sometimes, when pain and weakness lessen a little, to fight among the unseen forces of the field. Never, never is he shelved as of no further use to his Beloved Captain. To feel so, even for a moment, is to be terribly weakened and disappointed; for, like these young recruits to our Fellowship, did he not say from his first hour, "Swords drawn, up to the gates of heaven"? And did not his Captain accept and enroll him, mere foot soldier in the ranks though he be, and is he not still following the Colors? Blessed be the Lord of hosts, Captain and Leader of all fighting men—it must be so, it *is* so: it can never be otherwise. Only, as I have been learning through these months, the soldier must let his Captain say where, and for what, He needs him most, and he must not cloud his mind with questions. A wise master never wastes his servant's time, nor a commander his soldier's—there is great comfort in remembering that.

So let us settle it once for all and find heart's ease in doing so. There is no discharge in our warfare—no, not for a single day. We are never *hors de combat*. We may be called to serve on the visible field, going continually into the invisible both to renew our strength and to fight the kind of battle that can be fought only there. Or we may be called off the visible altogether for awhile, and drawn deep into the invisible. That dreary word "laid aside" is never for us; we are soldiers of the King of kings. Soldiers are not shelved.

O SAVIOUR Christ, who could forget
The crown of thorns, the tortured hours?
But on Thy brow there shall be set
A crown of fadeless flowers.

And may we bring our flowers to crown
The love that won at Calvary?
Down in the grass they grow, low down,
The least of flowers that be.

Immortal Love, Thy sun and showers
Have swept our field; O take Thine own,
Thy little flowers, Thy love's own flowers,
Dear Lord, to make Thy crown.

5. HOW SONGS CAME

THEY came not of set purpose, but because I could not help "taking" them, as the children say (they always think of songs, and music too, as something for which we put out our hand, as it were, and "take"). They are short, for when one is in pain one does not want much of anything; and I have so often been helped by the merest little morsel of song from some small bird in the garden, that I thought perhaps the ill, to whom these letters go, might find a minute's comfort or refreshment in something as simple and brief.

We have a little bird who has the pleasant custom of turning disturbing things into a cause for singing. The wind blows his bough and wakens him at midnight. His whole world is moving restlessly; he sings a tiny note or two then, perhaps to comfort himself. It is good to learn to do that.

Sometimes a song has come like coolness at the close of a hot day. The usual prayer-meeting of the Fellowship was going on in a room near mine. I could hear the singing, it was always comforting, but I could hear only the murmur of voices between prayer-songs and choruses; I did greatly long to be with my family then, and the filmy cloud of wish threatened to spread over my sky. It had been such a sudden swing out of the life which had been very life to me for so many years, and I had not got accustomed to the change (nor have I yet, eleven months after that first sudden closing down of all joyous activities). I was turning over the pages of an old book, not with much brightness of spirit, but as a distraction from desire, when I came upon this, "On Himself shall His crown flourish" ("blossom" is Delitzsch's word), "ever inflorescent, as a flower."

A blossoming crown—it was a delicately lovely little thought that floated into my room just then. It was like a flower or the petal of a flower blown in on a light wind. They made His crown of thorns on that woeful day on Calvary, but He will be crowned with flowers one day. Perhaps some of them must be gathered on the fiery fields of pain.

But there were days when the throb of the fleshly battle wound was lost in the sense of the throb of drums, as though heard from a long way off. Sometimes this victorious sound seemed to fill the air, and I all but saw the kingdoms of this world become the kingdoms of Christ our Lord. And songs came then about trumpets and bugles sounding afar, and about the triumph of our glorious King. Is it not a thought of exultation, that however crushed and crippled we may be, our Leader is marching to music all the time, marching to a victory sure as the eternal heavens? We follow a Conqueror. We prisoners of the Lord follow hard after Him as He goes forth to His Coronation. It is only our bodies that are bound. Our souls are free.

So the songs came. For by reason of the "interior sweetness," as Richard Rolle says, "I was impelled to sing what before I had only said" to Him who hears the least little song of love. Such a song need not look for words, though sometimes the search for the right word can be strangely refreshing. Songs without words are songs to Him.

"I COULD not see
  For the glory of that light,"
Let the shining of that glory
  Illumine our sight.

Things temporal
  Are transparent in that air,
But the things that are eternal
  Are manifest there.

Jesus, my Lord,
  By the virtue of Thy grace,
In the shining of Thy glory
  Let us see Thy face.

And a light shined in the cell,
And there was not any wall,
And there was no dark at all,
Only Thou, Emmanuel.

Light of Love shined in the cell,
Turned to gold the iron bars,
Opened windows to the stars,
Peace stood there as sentinel.

Dearest Lord, how can it be
That Thou art so kind to me?
Love is shining in my cell,
Jesus, my Emmanuel.

6. I COULD NOT SEE

IN the room where I am, a net curtain hangs over a door opposite to which my bed is set. The big protective cradle at the foot of the bed hides half of the curtain, but I can see the upper part, and on a day when there is not much light on the other side every fold in the curtain shows. But when the sun is shining on the green trees outside, then I can hardly see the net. It is there, but I cannot see for the glory of that light. This was continually a word of vision. The material, temporal details of that which I thought of as fetters of iron remained. There was no removing or evading them; and the old way (that of ignoring, treading under, things of the body) was impossible now. But there was a world that was nearer than the material. Things temporal are transparent in that air. Only *there* can one's spirit breathe and be strong.

And then this came from Switzerland, from the mother of the Matron of the Samaden Hospital (who had offered to our Fellowship). She had heard of this mauve curtain and of its message to me. "I should like to enlarge upon it a little," she wrote. "My father was a manufacturer, and once he gave me lengths of black and of white net. When my husband became a clergyman in a rural village we had to defend ourselves against mosquitoes, so we put the white net on frames. The result seemed excellent to us; when the light was unfavourable there was only a dim haze between the room and outside, and with a bright light even this was lost. But in time the net wore out, and to our regret we had only the black net to replace it. But with the black net one could see through clearly in every kind of light, so that we often hit our heads against the net when we wanted to look out of the window because we had forgotten it altogether.

"In the night the stars shine, and beyond the Cross the love of God shines; our earthly sadness, too, will be lost in the Light of Jesus."

Soon after this Swiss letter a cable from Australia brought us Acts 12:7 R.V., "And a light shined in the cell." It was such an endearing little word that it went of itself into song, as the glory of the light behind the curtain had. For that, one of our Fellowship, he whose music had so often solaced painful days, had "taken" a tune like wind in trees. Now another, the dear companion of many happy years, "took" music for the light in the cell. These two songs, often sung to me, continually brought to mind the many who have not such tender comforts. But their singing days will come, and their shining days too. For to all the children of the Father of Lights, however shadowed life may be, there is, there will be, "the light that changes all things."

HOME of our hearts, lest we forget
  What our redemption meant to Thee,
Let our most reverent thought be set
  Upon Thy Calvary.

We, when we suffer, turn and toss
  And seek for ease, and seek again;
But Thou upon Thy bitter cross
  Wast firmly fixed in pain.

And in our night star-clusters shine,
  Flowers comfort us and joy of song.
Nor star, nor flower, nor song was Thine,
  But darkness three hours long.

We in our lesser mystery,
  Of lingering ill and wingèd death,
Would fain see clear; but could we see,
  What need would be for faith?

O Lord beloved, Thy Calvary
  Stills all our questions. Come, oh come,
Where children wandering wearily
  Have not yet found their home.

7. FIXED IN PAIN

VERY early on in the course of events I prayed for one and only one thing (leaving to my family all prayer for healing; this was different). I prayed that power to cover signs of pain might be given, so that no one coming into the room should be saddened. But the effort sometimes required to suppress those signs led to something unexpected. I had never before realized how terrible it must have been for our Saviour to be fixed in one position, and that position one which was intolerably agonizing. He had not the help of movement, or of being moved.

It was, indeed, only a fraction of His piled-up suffering that was thus made vivid, but though it was only like a grain of the dust of that mountain, it was a real grain. The thought of it sent me to read the Gospels again and again, and as I pondered that Atoning Sacrifice, the magnitude of the cost to the Father, who so loved that He gave Him, was made just a little clearer, and the blessed, adorable love of our Lord Jesus, who, through the Eternal Spirit, offered Himself (but who can fathom those words?), became more real too.

Will this reach one who does not know Him?

Apart from Calvary, life is chaos, a confusion of distress, a black, deep horror of torment for all who are suffering severely, or who look through the thin skin of ice on the face of life to the black deeps below. To come to Him, the Supreme Sufferer, our Redeemer, to say to Him,

> Just as I am, without one plea
> But that Thy blood was shed for me,
> And that Thou bidd'st me come to Thee,
> O Lamb of God, I come,

is to find pardon, peace, heart rest. For the word is eternally true, "Come unto Me, all ye that labour and are heavy laden, and I will give you rest."

> None other Lamb, none other Name,
> None other hope in heaven or earth or sea,
> None other hiding-place from guilt and shame,
>   None beside Thee.
>
> My faith burns low, my hope burns low;
> Only my heart's desire cries out in me
> By the deep thunder of its want and woe,
>   Cries out to Thee.
>
> Lord, Thou art life, though I be dead;
> Love's fire Thou art, however cold I be:
> Nor heaven have I, nor place to lay my head,
>   Nor home, but Thee.

These beautiful words, Christina Rossetti's, say all that I want to say.

LOVER of souls, Thee have I heard,
  Thee will I sing, for sing I must;
Thy good and comfortable word
  Hath raised my spirit from the dust.

In dusty ways my feet had strayed,
  And foolish fears laid hold on me,
Until what time I was afraid
  I suddenly remembered Thee.

Remembering Thee, I straight forgot
  What otherwhile had troubled me;
It was as though it all were not,
  I only was aware of Thee.

And quietness around me fell,
  And Thou didst speak; my spirit heard;
I worshiped and rejoiced; for well
  I knew Thy comfortable word.

Whoso hath known that comforting,
  The inward touch that maketh whole,
How can he ever choose but sing
  To Thee, O Lover of his soul?

8. ROSE FROM BRIER

"I HAVE no desire that my imprisonment should end before the right time; I love my chains. My senses, indeed, have not any relish for such things, but my heart is separated from them and borne over them."

Madame Guyon said that. I cannot say that I love my chains in any literal sense whatever, nor do I feel that we are meant to do so. Our Lord did not tell the woman who was bound, to love the cords that bound her. But in the sense I am sure Madame Guyon meant the words (for, as she said, her senses had no relish for such things) I believe that He can give it to us to find something truly lovable in that which (while He allows it to continue) is His will for us.

Disappointments, for example; in a quiet procession these weary little things have entered this room. After the foot began to mend other troubles came, one after the other, pulling me up just when it seemed as though I might soon begin to walk. As each corner was turned we thought it would be the last, but there was always another.

But one of the first of these disappointments was lighted by something so sweet and dear that I knew at once it could not be only for me, but must be for you who know so very much more than I do of such matters.

One of our Fellowship was at home on furlough, and he was to return to us on February 25; I had set my heart on being up and ready to meet him and the new brother (of "Swords drawn") whom he was bringing with him. I was sure that I should be at the Welcome Service when that song was to be sung, for a month or so before that date it had seemed that this would be. Then the hope gradually faded. I was still in bed when they came, not even in a chair.

That morning, while the chiming bells of welcome were being rung from the tower, I was far more in the midst of that beloved crowd in the House of Prayer than here. And I ached to be there really, not just in spirit—ached till everything was one ache; and then, each word as clear as though it slid down the clear chiming bells, this little song sang within me:

Thou hast not *that,* My child, but Thou hast Me,
And am not I alone enough for thee?
I know it all, know how thy heart was set
Upon this joy which is not given yet.

And well I know how through the wistful days
Thou walkest all the dear familiar ways,
As unregarded as a breath of air,
But there in love and longing, always there.

I know it all; but from thy brier shall blow
A rose for others. If it were not so
I would have told thee. Come, then, say to Me,
My Lord, my Love, I am content with Thee.

"From thy brier shall blow a rose for others." In the hills of South India there are tall and beautiful bushes of wild roses. The roses are larger than ours at home and of an unforgettable sweetness. But they were not called to mind by these words. I saw rather a little, low, very prickly bush in an old-fashioned English garden; it was covered with inconspicuous pink roses. But the wonder of the bush was its all-pervading fragrance, for it was a sweetbrier. And I saw one who has long been in the land where no thorns grow, cutting a spray from the bush, stripping the thorns off and giving it to me. May these for whom a rose from my brier may be caused to blow, these who do indeed walk the dear familiar ways of home, and road, and street, as unregarded as a breath of air, but there in love and longing, always there, find no pricking thorn on the stem of this rose from my brier.

I think that when He whom our soul loveth comes so near to us, and so gently helps our human weakness, then what Madame Guyon wrote nearly three hundred years ago becomes a present truth. We are borne over the oppression that would hold us down, we mount up on wings, we find a secret sweetness in our brier. But it is not of us. It is Love that lifts us up. It is Love that is the sweetness.

Is the one who reads this in a great weariness, or the exhaustion that follows a sore hurt, or in the terrible grasp of pain? He who loves as no one else can love, who understands to the uttermost, is not far away. He wants us to say, He can give it to us to say, "My Lord, my Love, I am content with Thee."

Do Thou for me, O God the Lord,
　　Do Thou for me;
I need not toil to find the word
　　That carefully
Unfolds my prayer and offers it,
　　My God, to Thee.

It is enough that Thou wilt do,
　　And wilt not tire,
Wilt lead by cloud, all the night through
　　By light of fire,
Till Thou has perfected in me
　　Thy heart's desire.

O blessed be the love that bears
　　The burden now,
The love that frames our very prayers,
　　Well knowing how
To coin our gold; O God the Lord,
　　Do Thou, do Thou.

9. DO THOU FOR ME

I WROTE before of a soldier being removed to another part of the field when he is wounded—to a field hospital, so to speak, not a shelf—and of how, as pain lessens, one may fight among the unseen forces, joining with the angels and all the powers of Good, joining with our Lord Himself, who ever liveth to make intercession.

But I have not found myself that illness makes prayer easier, nor do any of our family who have been ill tell me that they have found it so. Prayerfulness does not seem to be a flower of the spirit that grows of itself. When we are well perhaps we rather take it for granted that it does, as though what is sometimes called a "sick-bed" offered natural soil for that precious flower. I do not think that it does. A bed can be a place of dullness of spirit as well as of body, and prayer is, after all, work—the most strenuous work in all the world. And yet it is our only way of joining the fighting force (we have declined the easy laid-aside cracked-china view of the matter). So what can we do about it?

One night, soon after neuritis had taken possession of me from shoulder blade to fingertips, I could no more gather myself up to pray than I could turn in bed without the help of the Lotus Bud, who was my faithful night-nurse. But I could read, and I opened on Psalm 109.

"Do Thou for me, O God the Lord." Do what? It does not say. It just says, *Do Thou for me.*

And the prayer, so simple, so easy for a tired heart, had a delivering power. It delivered from the oppression of the enemy. "Now there was leaning on Jesus' bosom one of His disciples, whom Jesus loved"; it was like that.

And soon the prayer passed into the most restful kind of intercession, the only kind the ill can attain unto, for they cannot pray in detail and they may know little or nothing of the needs of their dearest. But He knows all, down to the smallest wish of the heart. So we do not need to coin our gold in words, we could not if we tried: we are far too tired for that; and He who knows our frame does not ask us to do anything so arduous: Do Thou for her, do Thou for him, do Thou for them, O God the Lord.

This word of peace had greatly eased my spirit, when a letter came from the Secretary of the Dohnavur Fellowship Invalids' League.* She quoted from the letter of a Danish invalid too ill to pray as she longed to do: "This form of illness is very sad; but I am sure that God will learn His children in such times to have all their joy in God alone and not in the service for Him, not in their own forces. Of course you are thankful for these things also; *but the heart of*

---

*Interested persons may write to the London address given on page 200.

a child of God must be so, that God Himself is enough for it."

Was ever a deep truth more simply and beautifully spoken? Perhaps the word is meant for more than the ill. It is a word for all to whom He is the Best Beloved.

There was another night when, reading again in the Psalms, I discovered (I had not noticed it before) that the prayer, "Lord, all my desire is before Thee," was first prayed by a sick man: "Lord, all my desire is before Thee, and my groaning is not hid from Thee."

Next morning I was not able to write the usual note to my scattered family. (Before the accident I had usually had a few minutes with some of them at early morning tea between 6:30 and 7. After that interruption I sent them, when I could, a word which had fed me; and this grew into sharing my pot of manna with the larger family.) But the good angel of this peaceful room hung a picture of a bluebell wood on the front of the low chair on whose seat my feet rested. It is there now, a continual pleasure. The delicious green of young beech is seen against a pale sky; the blue of the bluebells rises like a softly murmured prayer ("Understand Thou my softly murmured prayer" is Rotherham's rendering of Psalm 5:1), or like the silence of love that lays its desire before its Beloved and leaves it there. Perhaps the little Song of Content that came singing through the bluebell wood that morning may have something for others also, like the rose on the sweetbrier:

As the misty bluebell wood,
  Very still and shadowy,
Does not seek for or compel
Several word from several bell,
But lifts up her quiet blue—
  So all my desire is before Thee.

For the prayer of human hearts
  In the shadow of the Tree,
Various as the various flowers,
Blown by wind and wet by showers,
Rests at last in silent love—
  Lord, all my desire is before Thee.

"In the shadow of the Tree"; the daffodils, that came before the bluebells, danced in the blessed sunshine. We have had daffodil days. If now for a season we are set like the bluebells in a shadowy place, that shade can only be the shadow of the Tree. "I sat down under His Shadow with great delight, and His fruit was sweet to my taste." Do the words seem too rapturous to be quite true? O Lord, Thou knowest; Lord, all my desire is before Thee.

O LITTLE bird that sings
Long before the glad day springs,
What radiant victory
You show to me.

You sing of conquering faith,
And of life subduing death,
And of joy before the light
Has vanquished night.

God of the sweet bird-song,
Let us all be borne along
By this triumphant mirth
That is not of earth.

Foreseeing dawn, would we
Now exult melodiously,
And sing before the light
Has vanquished night.

10. I WILL RENEW THEE IN MY LOVE

BUT there are times when we feel too tired even to desire; nothing is left in us to be refreshed; virtue has gone out of us. Will it ever come back? Can fatigue annihilate that which used to be, that resilience that so often has saved us from collapse? To be wakened by pain long before we should awaken, in spite of all that has been done to give us sleep, is to know that feeling. At such times the infantile bird-song which faces this letter has been a solace.

From mid-January till the cares of a family become too insistent, the magpie robin, a gay little bird in tidy black and white, sings before the dawn, sometimes as early as three o'clock. A long sustained sweetness suddenly breaks through the darkness, and drops of silver song are scattered everywhere. You lie listening gratefully, and your "Oh, how tired I am!" becomes of itself, "O little bird that sings"—which is at least happier than the other.

But not even the memory of that silvery sweetness can carry us through the day. Nothing but the very word of God made vital to the heart can do that. I wonder if this will do for another what it has done for me? The Septuagint rendering of Zephaniah 3:17,

"He will rest in His love," is, "He will renew thee in His love." There is enchantment in that word. There is life. There is strength.

> O God, renew us in Thy love to-day,
>   For our to-morrow we have not a care,
> Who blessed our yesterday
>   Will meet us there.
>
> But our to-day is all athirst for Thee;
>   Come in the stillness, O Thou heavenly Dew,
> Come Thou to us—to me——

September, on the south-eastern coast of India, is a burnt-up month. Round about Dohnavur the earth is terra-cotta colored and asks for the relief of low-growing green things; it can glare hotly when all that grows low is brown. The henna, within view of my window (henna is the camphire of the Song of Songs, "My Beloved is to me like a cluster of henna"), is then bare brown twig; the creamy, scented clusters are a mere memory; the little butterfly, caesalpinia, is a flicker of gold on unhappy stalks; frangipani, the temple flower, breaks out in strong blossom from a naked fat finger-stem, and the flame of the forest is all flame and no forest green.

But this year it is different, and this morning my chair was turned so that I could see into the enclosure upon which my room opens, and till the sun rose and made it too bright I feasted my eyes on the greenness. Never before have these eyes seen a green September. This year, the first time within living memory, not only are the greater trees, and of course all the palms, green (that is their happy custom), but the little henna is green, the gaiety of the caesalpinia is set in green, the temple-tree flowers are like pale stars in a green night, the gorgeous crimson of the forest flame glows bright from among its own gracious foliage. Rioting over a tangle of low bushes near my window the delicate large bells of the blue convolvulus call to the little sunbirds, and those lovely things, iridescent jewels in feathers, peck through the tube from the outside, poised in the air on tiny fluttering wings. Beside me is a fernball, lately achieved after many a vain essay; the mass of fragile lace is full of the whispers of woods and water. The unwonted beauty is because this year we have had rain during the hot weather; the sap is racing up every growing thing as though the thermometer did not register between 90 and 100 in the shade.

And all this sweet greenness and the dewy freshness of flowers is like a picture in color, set to familiar words. Leaves and flowers, down to the least leaf bud and flower bud, are nourished by the living sap. They do not cause it to rise, or regulate its flow. They do not understand its mysterious power. But as it flows through them it revives them, renews them. We who are ill know that we could never do much to bring the sap of life to bear upon our souls. We may have helps (I have, and they are countless), or we may have none (some have very few); but whether we are set in families or are as lonely as a sparrow on a housetop—that friendliest of little birds who does not like to be alone anywhere—we know that we depend on something that is not of ourselves to keep

us fresh and green. And we know that we are sometimes too spent even to pray for it.

We need not pray. There are times when all that is
asked of us is just what is asked of the leaves and
flowers and the fronds of the fern. They continue in
the plant, the sap flows up to them.

Continue ye in My love. The most tired of us can
continue, stay there, be there—no words can be too
simple to say what He means. Do not go away, He
says. Why should we? How could we? Do we want to
speak to Him? "He then lying on Jesus' breast saith
unto Him." Are we too tired to speak at all? Be silent,
then, in love. "Surely towards God silence becometh
my soul; from Him is mine expectation," is
Rotherham's rendering of Psalm 62: 1, 5. And as we
are silent, letting our hearts rest in quietness in Him
from whom is our expectation, He will cause the sap
to rise. He will renew us in His love. And so, however weary the clogging flesh may be, we shall win
through and we shall know,

> Patience of comfort, peace and fortitude,
> Drink where fresh waters flow,
> Taste angels' food.
>   For loving, Thou dost love until the end;
>   O great and dear Renewer, we have proved
>   What Love Divine can spend
>   On its beloved.

The things we would least choose to have are round
about us. But "In these things be not thrown down,
nor despair not; but stand evenly at the will of God,
and suffer all things that come to thee, to the praising

of our Lord Jesus Christ; for after winter cometh summer, and after even cometh day, and after tempest cometh clearness."

MAKE me to be Thy happy mountaineer,
   O God most high;
My climbing soul would welcome the austere:
   Lord, crucify
On rock or scree, ice-cliff or field of snow,
   The softness that would sink to things below.

Thou art my Guide; where Thy sure feet have trod
   Shall mine be set;
Thy lightest word my law of life, O God;
   Lest I forget,
And slip and fall, teach me to do Thy will,
   Thy mountaineer upon Thy holy hill.

It seemeth them also that they stand in their good peace when all things fall after their will and their feeling. And if it fall otherwise than they desire, they are soon moved and sorry.

Ofttimes it is need of spirit whereof the wretched body so lightly complaineth.

All Christ's life was a cross and a martyrdom; and thou seekest to thyself rest and joy?

The Imitation.

11. EVEREST

A NEW Everest Expedition—so the weekly *Times* of September 8. I have been reading Sir Francis Younghusband. He asks and answers the stock question, Who will be one ounce the better for it? This is part of his answer:

> And not only for mountaineering will the standard be raised, but for other fields of human activity as well. Many who have never been near a mountain have been thrilled by descriptions of the climbers' efforts to reach the summit, and have been spurred on by them to higher achievement in their own. So much has been proved by actual cases just as surely as any experiment in a laboratory.
>
> Everest has become a symbol. Everest stands for all that is highest, purest, and most difficult of attainment. As the climbers struggle gasping towards the summit they will be putting heart into all who are striving upward in whatever field. This knowledge will do most to put heart into themselves. So, in the words of Somervell, written on the day after his splendid failure: "The fight is worth it—worth it every time."

This carries me back to Neyyoor and the days and

nights when I lay reading the Everest books, not for
the first time; and especially when one day Dr. Somervell, the climber who spoke those valiant words
about the "splendid failure," made the pictures in
those books live, as only one could who had been
inside them himself (and, incidentally, drawn and
painted some of them). That story challenged me
then and it does again. True valor lies, not in what the
world calls success, but in the dogged going on when
everything in the man says Stop. That is the under-
note of those books; the refusal of softness, that is
what gripped me in the story.

Let us face it now: which is harder, to be well and
doing things, or to be ill and bearing things? It was a
long time before I saw the comfort that is in that
question. Here we may find our opportunity to
crucify that cowardly thing, the softness that would
sink to things below, self-pity, dullness, selfishness,
ungrateful gloom.

On the morning when the climbers of the second
expedition were at their highest camp, there was a
question about going farther. The night before, Dr.
Somervell, who, like all the others, was worn by
tremendous toils, had read in his pocket Testament
from Colossians, "If ye then be risen with Christ,
seek those things which are above." In the translation
he was using, the words ran thus: *Aim at what is above.*
They were in his mind now as he looked at that
summit, so near but so far, and he and his companion
decided to go on climbing. They had to take five
breaths to every step, five in and five out, but that day
those two men got higher than man had ever gone

before without oxygen, for it was the day of the "splendid failure."

This little incident, unrecorded, of course, in any of the books written about that famous climb (though it seems to me to express all such endeavor in a single luminous phrase), came out by accident one day in talk. I was asking Dr. Somervell about that last day's struggle uphill, and he told me about his little pocket Testament and its word to him. I was well then, and never expected to be anything else, having, as I have told, earnestly asked of the Lord a quick going on when the time came, with no loitering by the way; but the word of that story was for another day. Often during these months it has come and spoken to me. It has shamed slackness and cowardice; it has set me climbing again.

TOO GREAT FOR THEE

AN angel touched me and he said to me,
The journey, pilgrim, is too great for thee,
But rise and eat and drink,
   Thy food is here,
   Thy Bread of life,
   Thy cruse of Water clear,
Drawn from the brook, that doth as yesterday
   Flow by the way.

And thou shalt go in strength of that pure food
Made thine by virtue of the sacred Rood,
Unto the Mount of God,
   Where thy Lord's face
   Shall shine on thee,
   On thee in thy low place,
Down at His Feet, who was thy Strength and Stay
   Through all the way.

     O Cake of Bread baken on coals of fire,
     Sharp fires of pain,
     O Water turned to Wine,
     The word is true, this food is daily mine;
     Then never can the journey be
     Too great for me.

12. THE ANGEL OF THE LORD CAME AGAIN THE SECOND TIME

BUT there were hours when I could not bear to hear that song of the mountaineer sung by the group of loving singers who so often sang to me, because I did not feel that I had attained; and I feared very much what old Samuel Rutherford calls tongue-grace and paper-grace. All these letters are written from the lower slopes of Everest.

I have told how it came to be a custom to share my pot of manna in the form of a short note. I did not know till lately that some had copied these notes from day to day. To turn over the leaves of such a notebook is like turning back the weeks and months and looking at the past days again. This is what I find soon after the comforting assurance came, "Upon thy brier shall blow a rose for others."

1 Kings 19: 7: And the angel of the Lord came again the second time, and touched him, and said, Arise and eat; because the journey is too great for thee.
Is it not good and comforting to know that the angel of the Lord came again the second time? We never reach the place where we pass beyond the compassion of our God: His compassions fail not; they are new every morning; never tiring of us, always strong for our help

There have been times for nearly all of us when we have felt the truth of the angel's word, "The journey is too great for thee"; but have we not always found the Bread of Life and the Water of Life ready for our sustenance? And in the strength of that meat we have gone on, and shall go on, even unto the Mount of God.

But the perplexing thing is that even after we have been comforted and strengthened we can feel quite weak and tired again, just as though we had never been fed on the blessed Cake of Bread, the Water turned to Wine. It is consoling to find that we are not alone there. That heavenly-minded book, *Revelations of Divine Love,* which has opened to me more than ever during these months, is refreshingly candid. After the anchoress, Julian of Norwich, had seen the fifteen Shewings that, falling fair and steadily, each following other, had gladdened her heart, she wrote: "And at the end all was close, and I saw no more. And soon I felt that I should live and languish; and anon my sickness came again: first in my head with a sound and a din, and suddenly all my body was fulfilled with sickness like as it was afore. And I was as barren and as dry as if I never had comfort but little. And as a wretched creature I moaned and cried for feeling of my bodily pains and for failing of comfort, spiritual and bodily."

But her courteous Lord did not leave her; the words of solace follow a little later: *Thou shalt not be overcome* was said full clearly and full mightily, for assuredness and comfort against all tribulations that may come. *He said not: Thou shalt not be tempested, thou shalt not be travailed, thou shalt not be afflicted; but*

He said: Thou shalt not be overcome. God willeth that we take heed to these words, and that we be ever strong in sure trust, in weal and woe. For He loveth and enjoyeth us, and so willeth He that we love and enjoy Him and mightily trust in Him; and all shall be well.

Blessed be the patience of our Lord, our dear-worthy Redeemer. The angel of the Lord came again the second time.

THY touch hath still its ancient power,
  Thy loving touch that healeth all;
And yet we wait from hour to hour,
  Nor see Thee come by evenfall.

We bow before Thy Calvary;
  The twilit hour shall find us dumb,
And unoffended, Lord, in Thee:
  It will be clear when Thou dost come.

13. HEREFOR SHOULD WE NOT BE IN HEAVINESS

"BUT sometimes it cometh to our mind that we have prayed long time, and yet we think to ourselves that we have not our asking. But herefor should we not be in heaviness. For I am sure, by our Lord's signifying, that either we abide a better time, or more grace or a better gift." So Julian of Norwich again. One of the better gifts is the sweetness of our daily manna, which when we can only gather a very little, a mere handful, is somehow caused to suffice so that we have no lack. A single thought of love opens out, like a bud opening into flower before our eyes, as, indeed, the large violet passion-flower of South India does, between nine and ten every morning, whether growing or in a bowl by one's bedside—and a wonderful thing it is to see. Another of the better gifts is the power which is all divine, not in the least of us, to acquiesce with true inward peace in that which our Lord allows to be, so that it is not an effort to be happy, we *are* happy, and our prayer is this: "Thy will be my will, and may my will ever follow Thy will, and accord to it in all wise. Be there to me one willing and one not willing with Thee; and let me not will nor nill but what Thou wilt or wilt not." Nothing is farther from our thoughts than the dreary words, submission, resignation. To stay there would be dismal indeed,

> And, Lord, with a song,
> Let my will
> Run all the day long
> With Thy will.

That is life as we wish to live it.

But I do not find that this position, that of unbroken peacefulness and inward song, is one which we can hope to hold unassailed. It is no soft arrangement of pillows, no easy chair. It is a fort in an enemy's country, and the foe is wise in assault and especially in surprise. And yet there can be nothing to fear, for it is not a place that we must keep, but a stronghold in which we are kept, if only, in the moment we are conscious of attack, we look "away unto our faith's Princely Leader and Perfecter, Jesus, who endured" (Rotherham's rendering of Hebrews 12: 2). He who endured can protect and maintain that of which He is Author and Finisher: "Peace I leave with you, My peace I give unto you: not as the world giveth, give I unto you. Let not your heart be troubled, neither let it be afraid."

This peace, no lesser, no other, is proof against the sharp stab of longing to be well again, and the fiery dart of the knowledge of burden laid on others—and this is, I think, the fieriest dart of all. The peace of God can keep us steady in the place where we most desire to dwell, so that we shall not shadow the lives of those who love us.

> If, in the paths of the world,
> Stones might have wounded thy feet,

Toil or dejection have tried
Thy spirit, of that we saw nothing.

Of that we saw nothing—how good if, by His blessed enabling, we should daily so receive His peace that others should see nothing of stone, thorn, toil, dejection, but find, when they come, only the gift of a great contentment, the restful peace of God.

THERE are two Bethlehems in the land,
  Two little Bethlehems there.
O Wise Men, do you understand
  To seek Him everywhere?
The heavenly Child lies holily,
The heavenly Child lies lowlily,
  No crown on His soft hair.

There are three crosses on the hill,
  Three dreadful crosses there.
And very dark and very chill
  The heavy shuddering air.
Is there a sign to show my Lord,
The sinner's Saviour, Heaven's Adored?
  'Tis He with thorn-crowned hair.

For in His lovely baby days
  Heaven's door was set ajar,
And angels flew through glimmering ways
  And lit a silver star.
No need for halo or for crown
To show the King of Love come down
  To dwell where sinners are.

But when He died upon the Rood
    (The King of Glory, He),
There was no star, there was no good,
  Nor any majesty.
  For diadem was only scorn,
A twisted, torturing crown of thorn—
  And it was all for me.

14. SET TO LILIES—INCENSE TREES

QUOTATIONS can be tiresome, but there is just a chance that what helped those early days may help another's first days of illness. So I copy again from the notebook.

The Bible is amazing. Continually things that differ as much as things can, are bound together by golden chains. "The altar of God . . . God my exceeding joy." "Although the fig tree shall not blossom . . . yet I will rejoice in the Lord." "Now in the place where He was crucified there was a garden"; and so on from Genesis to Revelation. The title of Psalm 80, R.V.M. has taken me out of this room into a new world this morning: *Set to lilies, a testimony.* The lily breaks through hard ground after rain. Psalm 80 is hard ground. It is full of the hardness of suffering with others or for others. All who have ever suffered with this suffering world of ours understand this Psalm. They have walked on this hard ground.*

But the lilies break through the hardness of that (as it appears) purposeless pain, with a sudden upspringing of

---

*A Bill for the protection of horses was, at the time of this note, before Parliament. *The Illustrated London News* had played its part by showing haunting pictures of the traffic, and we who care for animals were fighting the cruel spirit of the love of gain by prayer.

hope and joy: "And cause Thy face to shine; and we shall be saved." Not I—there is no selfishness here; we, Thy creation—we shall be saved.

Whatever form our dry ground may take at the moment, we can rejoice in our lilies and listen to their testimony. There is an end set to pain, to sin. The present order is not eternal. The day will come, and we shall see it, when the word will be, "Neither shall there be any more pain," and He whom our soul loveth shall be as the light of the morning, when the sun riseth, even a morning without clouds; as the tender grass springing out of the earth by clear shining after rain.

More than the sweetness of lilies springs from the hard ground. There is something that the name Hazarmaveth of Genesis 10: 26 now brings to mind.

I never thought that a pot of manna was stored away in that word till I read of Hadramaut (as the word is now) in Southern Arabia.

On the scorching face of that land are towns and cities built entirely of mud bricks (the forts and palaces run to five stories; there is a minaret 175 feet high). No one could explore this region till lately, but now, because of the good government of the Dutch in Java, to which island some of the people from Hadramaut went, friendliness has begun to be, and a few explorers, with the help of the Dutch Government's influence, have been able to travel there. Photographs show a blistered land, naked to the sun, covered for miles with sand, broken stones, or bare rock, almost waterless, almost treeless.

But one of the high roads of the Old World, the trade route from India and Persia to Egypt and Syria, and to other countries round the Mediterranean, ran through this Hazarmaveth, and "it supplied its own fragrant contribution to that ancient-world commerce, a contribution not great in extent but vast in significance." Incense trees grew along the barren plateaux and in the dry riverbeds. Merchants came from as far as Persia to find this precious gum. The frankincense and myrrh the wise men offered to our Saviour may have grown in that burning land, and that which gave fragrance to the ointment Mary poured upon His hair and His feet, and the spices that the women laid among the linen for His burying. But the chief thought with me today is that this substance, universal symbol of prayer, worship, and adoration, was found in such a place. There is a touch of wonder in that, as in all the thoughts of God.

Sooner or later we find ourselves in some Hazarmaveth of His appointment. We may miss the incense trees or we may find them. If we miss them we shall not find them anywhere else. Have we, who are now in Hazarmaveth (and the name means Valley of death, or Court of death), found our incense trees?

One day in the Madras Museum the Curator, who was showing our children all he could in a single wonder-filled afternoon, stopped before a sandalwood tree. They knew that tree and delighted in the scent of its wood. "Where do you think it grows?" Dr. Henderson asked the children. They thought of gardens by the riverside, of forests by the riverside, where the soil is dark and rich. "No," he said, "it grows in the very poorest soil."

One of the hottest of Hazarmaveths for all who are ill must be, I think, Christmas Day. On my second Christmas Day, apart in measure from my dear family, I found comfort in "taking" a new carol, which, unlike most carols, would look not only at Bethlehem, but also at Calvary. There are times when nothing holds the heart but a long, long look at Calvary. How very small anything that we are allowed to endure seems beside that Cross.

15. BLOW UPON MY GARDEN

"Awake, O north wind; and come, thou south; blow upon my garden that the spices thereof may flow out." I believe that the Lord of the garden is the Speaker here. It is not for us to call, "Awake, O north wind."

Long ago a child, wedged in between three grown-ups on a sofa, listened, astonished, to one of those great people questioning the rightness of a certain prayer in a hymn. "I do not think that we should pray, 'Send grief and pain,' " remarked this audacious Irishwoman. It was quite wrong, of course, for was not a hymnbook almost as inspired as the Bible? But the day came when the child understood. It is only those who have never tasted real grief, real pain, who would dare to pray like that. Nor would anyone who had endured anything worth calling pain call it "sweet." ("Sweet are Thy messengers, sweet their refrain," says the hymn. St. Paul called his thorn the messenger of Satan.) To suffer intensely in soul or in body is to see pain for what it is, a dominating and a fearful thing. You do not try to penetrate the mystery of its being so, or of its being at all—you are far too tired to do anything of that kind; nor do you at that moment exult. We do not read of our Lord exulting in bodily agony, and yet, because for eternal reasons pain was bound up with the fulfillment of His Father's will, He could say without a shadow of reservation, "I delight to do Thy will, O my God: yea, Thy law is within my heart."

Through the garden the north wind is blowing now. Receive it, O my soul. All sharpness, all hardness, the difficult, the undesired, refuse none of these things. Set the doors into the secret avenues of being wide open to north wind or to south.

In Southern India the wind is often hot, and a hot air rises like a burning breath from the ground. That is what gave a line to the song overleaf. Such a wind parches the spirit, drains it of vitality, sends it to seek some cool place, caring only to find a shadow from the heat. But be the wind scorching, or sharp and cold, it can only cause the spices of His garden to flow out. And often, have we not found it so? the Lord of the garden calls His south wind; and all the flowers know it is blowing, and are glad.

SHADOW and coolness, Lord, art Thou to me;
Cloud of my soul, lead on, I follow Thee.
What though the hot winds blow,
Fierce heat beat up below,
Fountains of water flow—
    Praise, praise to Thee.

Clearness and glory, Lord, art Thou to me;
Light of my soul, lead on, I follow Thee.
All through the moonless night,
Making its darkness bright,
Thou art my heavenly Light—
    Praise, praise to Thee.

Shadow and Shine art Thou, dear Lord, to me;
Pillar of Cloud and Fire, I follow Thee.
What though the way be long,
In Thee my heart is strong,
Thou art my joy, my song—
    Praise, praise to Thee.

16. FOR GREEN OF SPRING—GOLD

THE song that faces this letter belongs to a time of stress. But it was then, as never before, that we learned the meaning of these words, "Oh how great is Thy goodness, which Thou has laid up for them that fear Thee, which Thou hast wrought for them that trust in Thee before the sons of men." Goodness, the sum of the good which God has treasured up for our constant and ever-increasing enjoyment; so Delitzsch interprets the word.

One of my happy opportunities for discovering the goodness which is treasured up for us all lies in watching quietly, as the days and nights slip past, how in every moment of inmost need something, perhaps quite a little thing, occurs for my comfort. Sometimes before the trouble has had time to form, as though it just happened so, a word comes to meet it and banish it to its own country. (For it does not belong to ours; it is of the earth, earthly. We desire a better country, that is a heavenly, where there are no interruptions to peace.)

Only last night in Brother Lawrence I came "by chance" on this: "Those who have the gale of the Holy Spirit go forward even in sleep." No one but

He who is nearer than breathing knew how the many nights that had seemed wasted were standing up in a row staring at me reproachfully; at least, I felt as though they were. Not that it was sleep which had made those nights so barren; it was distraction. The ill who know how thoughts can scatter like a flock of silly sheep, and refuse to come at all, or come only to tangle in knots, or to stretch out in a single tense desire to go to sleep—all who have such nights will understand how that simple word from the simplest of God's saints carried peace. He who is so kind to us when we sleep will not be less kind to us when we cannot sleep. He will cause His wind to blow. We shall go forward, though we seem to ourselves to be drifting back; so does He deal with us, the least of His children, according unto His name: for sweet is His mercy.

And He had something more waiting for the morning. An envelope marked "Please return" came with an early cup of tea. It was a little type-written letter dated April 12, 1918:

Be at rest about the work. It is God's, not ours. May He not do as He will with His own work—supply it with what it seems to us to need so much, or denude it of just that? Yes, He may. (Is it not lawful for Me to do what I will with Mine own?) Lord, Thou mayest do as Thou wilt with Thine own. We trust Thee, we love Thee; the work is Thine, not ours at all. We can only give Thee what Thou givest us of strength, of wisdom, of ability for it. If Thou takest these powers from us and makest us weak, so that we cannot help the work, if our children must be left without what we long to give them, Lord, it is Thy matter, not ours.

My child, it has meant much for me to come to this. Let not your heart be troubled, neither let it be afraid.

"These are true words," I said to myself, and then I saw the signature, "Mother," and knew that I must have written them to my own child Arulai, when, fifteen years ago, she was held by illness from helping as she longed to do. There are more to serve the children now than there were then, but there are many more children to serve. A little eighteen-months-old baby, Flower of Love, had just passed on to the heavenly nursery, and though the young nurse was being comforted, He knew all about the mother-feelings that had come with the dawn. There is something that touches the heart in the unrebuking love of the Lord. He does not speak in the surprised tone human love easily might; He gently brings to mind some verse upon which we have rested many a time, or something one of His servants has said, or sometimes even a poor little word of our own, and then we hear Him say, "Live now in the spirit of that." With the letter was this prayer printed on a card, *My God, I offer Thee all my thoughts, words, actions, and sufferings this day, for all the intentions of Thy Divine heart.* But there are hours too weary to remember so much. And as many a night finds "Lighten our darkness" or some other long-loved word enough, so does many a dawn settle softly on something as simple as this: "O Lord Jesus, my Belovèd, let me be a joy to Thee." And a little prayer comes of itself for the dear nurses, that they may have a happy day; and for the family, too many to recall name by name, though face by face they pass before the heart that loves them all—"Do Thou for them, O God the Lord." Later there is always the manna, for when the dew fell upon the camp in the night, the manna fell upon it. Like the Lord of the manna, it is very readily found.

And there are books. I suppose we all have our own familiar book-friends, books that we could not do without. (How glad I should be if the little *Rose* might be that, even to only one.) Among mine I name very gratefully *The Pilgrim's Progress.* I do not think that we find the gathered wealth of truth and power and beauty in that book till we read it after life has had time to explain it. "But was a man in a mountain of ice, yet if the Sun of Righteousness will arise upon him, his frozen heart shall feel a thaw; and thus it hath been with me."

I chanced on this while I was thinking of the words *Quicken Thou me,* which had been as rain to very dry grass. Frozen heart, withered heart, all it needs is to meet the Look of its dear Lord. "And thus it hath been with me."

There are days when we can sing and feel that our leaf "shall not wither" ("doth not wither," as the R.V. has it)—watered-garden days. There are days when we feel like any old bit of dried-up grass in a dry and thirsty land where no water is. Blessed be God that the Bible is so human. When my heart is vexed, I will complain. ("That is not in the Bible," said somebody once, almost shocked at the idea that anything so extremely ordinary could be in that sacred Book. It was found, however, in the Prayer-Book Version of Psalm 77: 3.) Blessed be

God for the truthful Psalms.

So this word, Quicken Thou me, carries two streams of living water. Are we rejoicing in a sense of life? Then, Lord, keep that which Thou hast given. Are we dull, dead? Then, Lord, make us to live, as Thou usest to do unto those that love Thy Name—"According to the custom" (marginal reading). It is our Saviour's custom to do this for us. "Turn Thee unto me," we pray; He turns and looks, and in His look there is a quickening, and renewal of faith and love and courage. All is well again, for He has come—

How entered, by what secret stair,
I know not, knowing only He was there.

Sometimes He enters by way of a picture. One day, and it was one of the withered days, like the day when the bluebell wood spoke its restful word, a large parcel from Holland was carried into my room and carefully unpacked. It had been held up for some time at the customs because no one there knew what a *plaat* could be. It might have been a flat-shaped bomb. But here it was at last. And what a *plaat!* We saw a road bordered by horse chestnut trees in their autumn coloring. Ten magnificent trees on one side, nine on the other, their glowing glories of golden leaf filling the air, reflected in the pool on the road, melting into the misty blue of the distance where a shepherd drives his flock, scattering on the mossy cushions and the grass at the trees' foot their gold and golden brown, illuminating with bright touches the grey-green boles.

And, as once before in a forest by a waterfall, a

voice spoke to me saying, "Can I who do *this* not do *that?*" so now again a voice spoke, and this time through those noble trees, the work of His hands, and their heavenly wealth of beauty: "Can I who made the green of spring not do that for autumn? for thy vanished green, for thy vanished flowers, give gold?"

The jubilant thought of gold for green had just begun to sing within, when a magazine brought this:

> And then a little laughing prayer
>   Came running up the sky,
> Above the golden gutters, where
>   The sorry prayers go by.
> It had no fear of anything,
>   But in that holy place
> It found the very throne of God,
>   And smiled up in His face.

17. AS GLAD AND MERRY AS IT WAS
POSSIBLE

NEARLY five hundred years ago Julian of Norwich wrote that when she was earnestly thinking of our Lord's suffering, and trying to see (as it were) His dying,

> . . . suddenly, He changed the look of His blessed Countenance. The changing of His blessed Countenance changed mine, and I was as glad and merry as it was possible. Then brought our Lord merrily to my mind: "Where is now any point of the pain or of thy grief?" And I was full merry.

But this is only the beginning. It has not entered into the heart to conceive the joy that is drawing nearer every day—the joy that shall be ours when we are where there will be no more withering or fear of withering.

> I understood that we be now, in our Lord's meaning, in His Cross with Him in His pains and His passion, dying; and we, willingly abiding in the same Cross with His help and His grace unto the last point, suddenly He shall change His Cheer to us, and we shall be with Him in Heaven. Betwixt that one and that other shall be no

time, and then shall all be brought to joy. And thus said
He in this Shewing: "Where is now any point of thy pain
or thy grief?" And we shall be full blessed.

So she was "full merry." If it can be this now, what
will it be when (as we trust, shortly) we shall see Him,
and we shall speak face to face?

It seems to me clear beyond question that in the
lives of God's beloved there are sometimes periods
when the adversary is "given power to overcome."
This power need never overwhelm the inner courts
of the spirit, but it may press hard on the outworks of
being. And so I have been asking that our dearest
Lord may have the joy (surely it must be a joy to
Him) of saying about each one of us, and about us all
as a little company of His children: "I can count on
him, on her, on them for *anything*. I can count on
them for peace under any disappointment or series of
disappointments, under any strain. I can trust them
never to set limits, saying, 'Thus far, and no farther.' I
can trust them not to offer the reluctant obedience of
a doubtful faith, but to be as glad and merry as it is
possible."

And all that begins in the gift of a great contentment.

18. BEGINNING TO SINK . . . IMME-
DIATELY . . . .

BUT even so, for we are all weakness in ourselves, there are times when nothing comes to mind but these words. They assure us of so much more than they seem to say that their riches of comfort cannot be condensed into a page.

Chiefly they bring the certainty that there will be no sinking, for Peter never sank. ("When I said, My foot slippeth" in that very moment—"Thy mercy, O Lord, held me up.") They come underneath the feeling of sinking; they say, "This shall never be."

It was Christ's sorely tried prisoner, Samuel Rutherford, who wrote that the parings and crumbs of glory, a shower like a thin May-mist of his Lord's love, was enough to make him green and sappy and joyful. Such a word, even such a little word as this, if only we open our hearts to its healing power, may be a crumb of glory, enlightening the soul, a thin May-mist of His love making green and sappy (or glowing and golden) what was so dry and dull before.

"And immediately Jesus stretched forth His hand and caught him." How many seconds lie between a man's beginning to sink and his sinking? A single second or less, I suppose, sees one who is beginning to sink under water. How swift, then, was the movement of love! And as He was, so He is. "Must we wait till the evening to be forgiven?" a child asked once. Do we not all know that feeling? It seems too good to be true that at the very moment of the sorrowful consciousness of sin, or even the shadow of sin, there is pardon, cleansing, the light of His blessed Countenance. But nothing ever can be too good to be true with such a Lord as ours.

The use of that word "immediately" has been life and peace to me of late. They were troubled, those poor men in the boat. "And immediately He talked with them." We know what He said; He has said it to us often.

How needless their trouble seems to us as we read. Does ours seem as needless to the heavenly watchers? Do they wonder about us, as we do about those men, how there could be room for trouble in a ship that was under His command? (It was He who had constrained them to go to the other side. It is He who directs our boat now to the Other Side.) But there is nothing of this wonder in the sweetness of the words of our Lord Jesus when immediately He talked with them. He understood.

We who know (as I more than ever do now) how upholding dear and loving words can be, when a friend who understands does not blame, but just understands even the trouble that need not be, and comforts it—we can find honey in this honeycomb: "Immediately Jesus stretched forth His hand and caught him." "My soul hangeth upon Thee: Thy right hand upholdeth me." "Immediately He talked with them." "Speak, Lord: for Thy servant heareth."

19. WORMS

AND He talks with us in many ways, sometimes through the pleasure of rarely quoted lovely old words, like those from Herrick, who, when in 1647 his all was taken from him wrote

> God, when He takes my goods and chattels hence,
> Gives me a portion, giving patience:
> What is in God is God; if so it be
> He patience gives, He gives Himself to me.

But *Weigh Me the Fire* is what carries me far away from bed and chair to-day:

> Weigh me the fire; or canst thou find
> A way to measure out the wind;
> Distinguish all those floods that are
> Mixed in that watery theatre;
> And taste thou them as saltless there
> As in their channel first they were.
> Tell me the people that do keep
> Within the kingdoms of the deep;
> Or fetch me back that cloud again,
> Beshiver'd into seeds of rain;
> Tell me the motes, dust, sands, and spears
> Of corn, when summer shakes his ears;

Show me that world of stars, and whence
They noiseless spill their influence:
This if thou canst, then show me Him
That rides the glorious cherubim.

And yet, in spite of the help that is given, there is a
feeling (I can only call it worminess) that can come,
especially between 2 and 3 o'clock in the morning,
when all the fight seems to be drained out of us. It is
really a very horrid feeling, but the word of our God
is equal to anything—even to this. At such a time,
clear through the fug and stuffiness and the oppression of the enemy, the worminess, came this, *Fear
not, thou worm!*

It was startling; it was so exactly *it*. There was no
smooth saying that things were not as they were.
They were wormy. I was wormy. Well, then, "Fear
not"; He who loves us best knows us best; He meets
us just where we are. But He does not leave us there.
There is power in the word of the King to effect what
it commands. In the *Fear not* of our God (a word
repeated in one form or another from Genesis to
Revelation) there is power to endue with what at the
moment is most lacking in the one to whom it is
spoken, be it courage, or the will to endure and to
triumph which so easily slips away from us, or the
love that we need so much if we are to help others,
the love that never fails, or the wisdom which is not in
us, and which we must have if we are to make right
decisions, or just common hope and patience to carry
on in peace and joyfulness of spirit. O Lord, I am
nothing before Thee, a worm and no man. *Fear not,
thou worm.*

Fear not, thou worm Jacob . . . . I will help thee, saith the Lord thy Redeemer, the holy One of Israel, for I, thy God, am firmly grasping thy right hand—am saying unto thee, Do not fear; I have become thy helper. Do not fear, thou worm.

Do not fear, but sing: "Praise the Lord upon earth, mountains and all hills, fruitful trees and all cedars, beasts and all cattle, *worms*."

These various words helped me exceedingly. And yet I know that they may be dumb to some who turn the pages wearily, their strength spent out in the hot land of pain.

In one of Blackwood's *Tales from the Outposts* a man, telling of an arid tract of country in Central Africa, despairs of making one who has not experienced that flaming heat understand anything about it:

But how describe the thirst and heat of torrid lands to those who simply turn the tap near at hand to secure an endless cooling supply? How describe the thirst engendered by effort on foot across miles of stark, shadeless forest, heated by a ball of molten fire, to those who live in temperate, well-watered lands of perpetual verdure? The English language, born in a land of cloudy skies, frequent showers, forest shades and evergreen fields, with water on every side, lacks, and must lack, terms for precise description of heat, thirst and drought.

This writing lacks, and must lack, the precise touch that is granted only to one who has endured the devouring flame of an anguish that can lick up to the last drop the juice of life. I write from a cooler region than that of many a hospital ward and nursing home.

Should it find its way to one who is in the fiery waste, the lack that must be will be recognized. "She has not been here," the reader will say. "She does not understand." Knowing this, I have often laid aside the writing as a vain thing and presumptuous.

But He whose words have been as cool water to me in my lesser desert, did in His own flesh endure the extremity of thirst. We cannot say of Him, "He has not been there." He has been there, and He has not forgotten, nor will He ever forget, what it was to be there. We have not a high priest who cannot be touched with the feeling of our infirmities. Touched with the feeling—could words be more understanding? "Tempted in all points like as we are"—unrecorded experiences of suffering lie there. Able to succor them that are tempted—follow that single line of thought, it is like a track across a desert, and soon we come to deep wells of cool water: Whosoever drinks of that water shall never thirst. They thirsted not when He led them through the deserts.

Thus far the notebook. I have strung the quotations together without interspersing songs, lest too many singing birds should alight on the rosebush. And, after all, to each lover of the Lord are his own singing birds.

DEAR Lord, for all in pain
  We pray to Thee;
O come and smite again
  Thine enemy.

Give to Thy servants skill
  To soothe and bless,
And to the tired and ill
  Give quietness.

And, Lord, to those who know
  Pain may not cease,
Come near, that even so
  They may have peace.

And then sheweth our courteous Lord Himself to the soul—well-merrily and with glad cheer—with friendly welcoming as if it had been in pain and in prison, saying sweetly thus: *My darling, I am glad thou art come to me: in all thy woe I have ever been with thee; and now seest thou My loving, and we be oned in bliss.* Thus are sins forgiven by mercy and grace, and our soul is worshipfully received in joy like as it shall be when it cometh to Heaven, as often-times as it cometh by the gracious working of the Holy Ghost and the virtue of Christ's Passion.

JULIAN OF NORWICH.

20. BROWN-PAPER PARCELS

SOMETIMES our friends at home kindly slip into a box of Christmas things for the children a ball or two of silver or gold tinsel-tape or narrow ribbon, and perhaps a few sheets of tissue paper—things we should never dream of buying. Such friends have imagination. They know the pleasure of giving a daintily wrapped up gift. I think our Father, who does often give us the pleasure of receiving our heart's desire most beautifully wrapped up, must watch with special love in His eyes when His gifts come in common brown paper, apparently rather badly packed. Shall we find the precious things folded up inside or shall we be put off?

In the early morning of October 24, 1931, my thoughts went out to those who were about to join our Fellowship. I thought of our growing numbers, and of our children, so many of whom were entering the difficult years, and of the unwon caste Hindu and Muslim towns—the great Unreached of Southern India, and then back to our new recruits. And I did then earnestly ask to be prepared by any means, at any cost, to do more for them all. I cannot yet see how the thing that I asked that morning can possibly be inside this parcel. But perhaps when all the knots are untied, the string rolled up, the paper tidily folded away, I shall know. In the meantime another prayer has been shaping for the town where my brown-paper parcel was received. I am asking for a soul for each month spent in bonds. Of the few given already, two are safe in the Land of Light. The story of one of the two tells of a gift wrapped up in very rough brown paper.

The beginning takes us back to a day, two years ago, when we were praying for someone to reach the. Brahman and other high-caste men of Joyous City, who throughout their whole history had refused to take the slightest interest in the gospel. Caste-pride can build walls like the great double walls that surround our South Indian temples. For six years we had prayed to be able to rent a house in that antagonistic town. Now at last we had secured one. But we had no one who could reach the men. The day the key of the house was given to us an old man called on his way from one town to another, and as he looked tired we asked him to rest for the night.

Next day we knew that he was a Christian from the innermost fort of Brahmanism. His name was Triumph. For seven years he had sat as a disciple at the feet of a famous guru in Benares, but his search for peace was in vain. One day he came upon his teacher reading with tears from St. John 14. "Have you found what you have been seeking all these seven years in the *Védas*?" asked his guru; and to his sorrowful "No," his guru told him that he would never find it there; he would find it only in the gospel of our Lord Jesus Christ. He himself believed, he said, but feared to confess because of the reproach of the Cross. Together guru and disciple read the Pentateuch, Daniel, the Gospels and Revelation. For months they read, "till these eyes which were blind were opened, and I saw." But I cannot show the shining eyes of that old man, as he told of it, or the quick reminiscent gesture. Truly his eyes had seen. Nor can I tell you how glad we were as we gave him the key of the house of Joyous City, and knew (for he stayed on with us, most surely believing that he had been sent for this very reason) that at last there was one who could reach those men; and he lived among them for some months. Meanwhile I was laid in bonds, and somehow, I hardly know how, I finished *Gold Cord,* which had been begun three years before, and this story straight from life went into it.

But before the proofs came back our hopes had crashed. Diabetes, from which our friend had previously suffered, flared up, and the dry heat tried him. He became subject to strange delusions and could not any longer witness to his Lord. He returned to his own country on the other side of the mountains, and Joyous City was left without anyone who could reach the men. So a paragraph on page 347 had to be rewritten for the sake of that which matters most in a book—truth.

Months later a man with dysentery came to us from that little fortress of Caste, and with him were his wife and sister. A Muslim from Song of the Plough, the first won from that fort of Islam, found in him a heart prepared, and led him to our Lord. The little sister believed too. The sick man told then how Triumph had visited him, and had opened to him the love of his Redeemer, sowing in his heart the first seed of desire. A few days later, after receiving the assurance of forgiveness, he insisted on being taken to our House of Prayer, and there, in that crowded house, before all our family and some of his own indignant townsfolk who had come to see him, he witnessed to the glorious grace of the Lord. I find it hard to believe that I was not there, did not hear him; I was so much there in spirit that I all but heard that faint voice, saw that face, grey and worn with long illness, but so peaceful and so glad.

Shortly afterwards, a sudden madness seized him. He had been in perfect mental health up to that moment, and a whisper went round about "the mind-destroying drug in his coffee." His cries filled this room (for the Indian house used as a pro tem hospital is less than fifty yards from my room). Nothing could be done for him except that, if he were able to understand, prayer soothed him, the Name of our Lord Jesus comforted him. He was taken home at last; his little sister, alone among the deriding Hindus, held firm to her newly found Saviour; "I could not have borne it if He had not been there," she said.

But those were terrible days. Our young workers, who lived in a house near his, could hear the piteous cries. Were the powers of darkness shouting in triumph down the street? It seemed so to those who, alone but for their God, felt the encompassing darkness pressing and crushing like an evil force. Then the cries ceased. That redeemed soul was with its Lord. And all through, the brave little sister held fast to Him whom she believed, and was held fast by Him.

Prayer for anything that would make the one who was servant of all more able to serve—a disabling accident. Prayer for a soul to be saved for every month of battle-wound in the town for whose sake that hurt had been—illness of the only man who could reach the most opposed; death (as the whispers said, and as I who know the ways of this land believe, by some mind-destroying drug) of the first notable convert won—brown paper, rough string indeed. But we wait till the string is untied, the paper unfolded. Then what shall we see?

One prayer, whose answer has come wrapped in something softer to the touch, is this: we asked that the loving care of the children for their mother might lead them far past her, farther than they had ever gone before in truly effective prayer for others. I think that this prayer is being answered; for many to whom pain is as yet only a name are being led into ways of sympathy. And I trust that the Father has often sent and will often send help to doctor, nurse, patient, in other places, in answer, perhaps, to the prayer of one of our children, and give to him, to her, who knows "pain may not cease," His peace.

Lord, is all well? Oh, tell me; is all well?
  No voice of man can reassure the soul
  When over it the waves and billows roll;
His words are like the tinkling of a bell.
  Do *Thou* speak; is all well?

      Across the turmoil of the wind and sea,
      But as it seemed from somewhere near to me,
      A voice I know—*Child, look at Calvary;
      By the merits of My Blood, all is well.*

Whence came the voice? Lo, He is in the boat:
  Lord, wert Thou resting in Thy love when I,
  Faithless and fearful, broke into that cry?
O Lord, forgive; a shell would keep afloat
  Didst Thou make it Thy boat.

And now I hear Thy mighty "Peace, be still,"
  And wind and wave are calm, their fury, froth.
  Could wind or wave cause Thee to break Thy troth?
They are but servants to Thy sovereign will;
  Within me all is still.

Oh was there ever light on land or sea,
  Or ever sweetness of the morning air,
  Or ever clear blue gladness anywhere
Like this that flows from Love on Calvary—
  From Him who stilled the sea?

      Father and Son and Spirit be adored;
      Father, who gave to death our Blessed Lord;
      Spirit, who speaks through the Eternal Word,
      By the merits of the Blood, all is well.

21. IS ALL WELL?

THE story of the Lord at rest in the boat, and the disciples in fear disturbing that rest, is, I think, like an opal: it has a quiet little flame in its heart. Are there never times when the fear springs to life, Is all well? No voice of man could reassure us. We must have our Lord's, His very own. And so sometimes we have, as it were, broken in upon the Rest, the Silence of His love, with a needless cry. To such a cry He lately answered me in words which I shall hold fast, God helping me, for ever, "By the merits of My Blood, all is well."

Or the fear may be for that which is dearer to us than ourselves. (The dearer it is, the keener the temptation to the kind of fear that always lies alongside love.) All had gone well with the ship till suddenly there arose a great storm of wind, and the waves beat into the ship, so that it was now full. What of that beloved soul, how is it faring? or that work—but "work" is too cold a word for the living, loving thing which has been committed to us—what if suddenly a great storm should arise? So there is fear, devastating fear. And the more sensitive we are to the possibility of spiritual peril, the more urgent that fear can be, till it turns to a cry that cannot be restrained: "Master, Master, carest Thou not?"

It is a needless cry. "For I know whom I have believed, and am persuaded that He is able to keep that which I have committed unto Him against that day." Storms may lie ahead. The waves may break into the ship. There is no promise of a calm passage. Let us settle it, therefore, in our hearts, as something that cannot be shaken, that our first prayer, our deepest desire, shall be not for blue skies and sweet airs, but that we may always have the ungrieved Presence of the Captain and the Master in our ship. Lord Jesus, let us tolerate nothing that would keep Thee from resting in Thy love, come fair weather, come foul.

But we can be tormented by fear of failing before the end of the journey. We need not fear. It was George Tankervil, he who said,*

> Though the day be never so long
> At last it ringeth to evensong,

who, out of weakness, was made strong.

He so greatly feared lest he should flinch from martyrdom, that to test himself he had a fire kindled in the chamber where he was confined, and sitting on a form before it, he put off his shoes and hose and stretched out his foot to the flame; but when it touched his foot, "he quickly withdrew his leg, showing how the flesh did persuade him one way and the

*Perhaps quoting from Stephen Hawes who died before 1530. Tankervil was martyred in 1555.

Spirit another way." And yet a few hours later, when he came to the green place near the west end of St. Albans Abbey where the stake was set, he kneeled down, and when he had ended his prayer he arose with a joyful faith. Before they put the fire to him a certain knight went near and said softly, "Good brother, be strong in Christ." And he answered, "I am so. I thank God." So embracing the fire, he bathed himself in it, and calling on the name of the Lord, was quickly out of pain.

Have we not often been like George Tankervil? We have imagined what was coming, and perhaps tested our constancy by some fire of our own kindling, and faith and courage have suddenly collapsed. For grace to endure and to conquer is never given till the moment of need, but when that moment comes? O Saviour, who dost not forget Thy Calvary, hast Thou ever failed the soul that trusted Thee? Never, never. By the merits of Thy Blood all is well, all shall be well.

O THOU who art my quietness, my deep repose,
My rest from strife of tongues, my holy hill,
Fair is Thy pavilion, where I hold me still.
Back let them fall from me, my clamorous foes,
Confusions multiplied;
From crowding things of sense I flee, and in Thee
hide.
Until this tyranny be overpast
Thy hand will hold me fast;
What though the tumult of the storm increase,
Grant to Thy servant strength, O Lord, and bless
with peace.

As a family God has been speaking to us recently,
through the death of my youngest sister, Freda, on August
31. We have no details yet. She sailed on September 18 of
last year in one of the parties of the Two Hundred, after
ten years' patient waiting for the way to open.

Many of our friends in their letters of sympathy speak of
God's mysterious ways, and I know there is an element of
mystery. But I shrink from the suggestion that our Father
has done anything which needs to be explained. What He
has done is the best, because He has done it, and I pray that
as a family we may not cast about for explanations of the
mystery, but exult in the Holy Spirit, and say, "I thank
Thee, Father. . . . Even so, Father." It suggests a lack of
confidence in Him if we find it necessary to try to understand all He does.

Will it not bring Him greater joy to tell Him that we
need no explanation because we know Him? But I doubt
not there will be a fulfillment of John 12: 24

REV. FRANK HOUGHTON
(*China Inland Mission*): *From a letter.*

22. WE NEED NO EXPLANATION

OUR hearts rejoice in that word for so great a matter. It is, indeed, the only perfect word. But perhaps sometimes in an incomparably lesser trial the tempter has disturbed us by persuading us to look for an explanation. We find ourselves saying, I wonder why. *Faith never wonders why.*

Among our several hundred of all ages in the Dohnavur family who are being taught in the ways of prayer, there were many for whom this lesson was set when the answer to their prayers was "turned to the contrary" just as they thought they had safely received it. For on a certain evening there was special prayer for the healing touch, and that night the pain was lulled and natural sleep was given. The blissfulness of the awakening next morning is still vivid and shining. I lay for a few minutes almost wondering if I were still on earth. (No night has been like that since; no sleep like that has come, nor any such easeful wakening.) I knew something that morning of what it will be when He "shall look us out of pain."

And all the dear household rejoiced. Down to the tiniest child who could understand there was gladness and thanksgiving. Had they not asked for healing by the Touch of God? Was this not that? So they accepted it with a reverent and lovely joy. But my nurse was careful in her joy, and nothing was done, no carelessness occurred that could account for what followed. The pain returned and increased. The nights were as they had been. And some did, I know, find it very confusing and very disappointing. For was there not prayer? Indeed there was. The loving care of those who led the prayer of our Fellowship had divided the day into watches; there was never an unprayed-for hour. But the bars closed down once more. Was it strange that to some who have not known Him long, there was the trial of wondering "Why"?

"I am learning never to be disappointed, but to praise," Arnot of Central Africa wrote in his journal long ago—it was the word of peace to us then. I think it must hurt the tender love of our Father when we press for reasons for His dealings with us, as though He were not Love, as though not He but another chose our inheritance for us, and as though what He chose to allow could be less than the very best and dearest that Love Eternal had to give. But on a day of more than a little trial, in His great compassion I was allowed to see—for as the ear is unsealed at times, so are the eyes opened—and I knew that the enemy had asked to be allowed to recover his power to oppress, and that leave had been granted to him, but within limits. I was not shown what those limits were; I saw only the mercy that embraces us on every side. Was that moment of insight merely a pale reflection of an ancient familiar story? So some will understand it.

But the comfort that comes through such a moment never stays to argue about itself. It sinks deep into the heart and gives it rest. Thereafter, not seeing, not hearing, not feeling, we walk by faith, finding our comfort not in the thing seen or heard in that illuminated moment (though, indeed, that which was seen or heard does, with a sweetness peculiar to itself, continue to console), but in the Scriptures of truth: "I know whom I have believed, and am persuaded that He is able to keep that which I have committed unto Him against that day. . . . And we know that all things work together for good to them that love God." With Him who assures us of this there is no variableness, neither shadow that is cast by turning. His word stands true. In that truth we abide satisfied.

> Until this tyranny be overpast,
> Thy hand will hold me fast.

And so I have come to this: our Lord is sovereign. He may heal as He will, by an invisible Touch or by blessing the means (His gifts) that are used. He may recover the exhausted one, as Rotherham renders James 5: 15, or sustain with words him that is weary, as He did St. Paul, and use those words for the succor of others.

"But you are not St. Paul": I remember reading that in a book on healing, just after I had been given peace in acceptance of a certain thorn in the flesh. I had prayed more than three times that it might depart from me, but it had not departed. "You are not St.

Paul." It was true, of course, but it seemed too facile to be a true answer to this riddle of the universe.

And now, the more I study life as well as books, the more sure I am that there is a darkness folded round that riddle into whose heart of light we are not meant to see. Perhaps that light would be too bright for our eyes now. I have known lovers of our Lord who in their spiritual youth were sure beyond a doubt that healing would always follow the prayer of faith and the anointing of oil in the name of the Lord. But those same dear lovers, in their beautiful maturity, passed through illness, unrelieved by any healing. And when I looked in wonder, remembering all that they had held and taught in other years, I found them utterly at rest. The secret of their Lord was with them. He had said to them, their own beloved Lord had said it, "Let not your heart be troubled, neither let it be afraid"; so their hearts were not troubled or afraid, and their song was always of the lovingkindness of the Lord. "As for God, His way is perfect," they said. "We need no explanation."

Today with this thought in mind I read the Song of the Redeemed, the ninth song St. John heard after a door was opened in heaven: "Great and marvellous are Thy works, Lord God Almighty; just and true are Thy ways, Thou King of saints." Some of us cannot enter fully into even earthly music until it has become familiar. Perhaps our various experiences here are means by which we may learn the heavenly melody to which such words are set, so that when we hear the harpers harping on the harps of God we shall catch the thread of that melody, and follow it through its harmonies, moving among them with confidence and gladness as on familiar ground. *As for God, His way is perfect*—that is the substance of the words. And if His way be perfect we need no explanation.

O WOUNDED feet, O famished eyes,
  Is there no healing anodyne?
No spell to make the wayworn wise?
  No hint of the Divine?
But if indeed we too might bear
  The Dying of the Blessed One;
But if indeed we too might wear
  The Life of God's dear Son,
Oh would we, could we, choose to miss
  For loveliest bud of garden born,
One blow of reed, one stab from this
  Our Saviour's crown of thorn?

    *   *   *   *   *

There is a touch, there is a spell,
  There is a healing anodyne;
Not far art Thou, Emmanuel,
  From troubled child of Thine.
O Master of the wounded feet,
  From whose sharp crown the red dew fell,
And would I walk mid meadow-sweet,
  Crowned with gold asphodel?

23. WE BRING OUR LOVE TO THEE

I SUPPOSE that in the lives of all our Lord's lovers
there are memories of an hour when earth and time
and sense fell far away, and they saw only Calvary,
felt only Love—Love that burned as nothing save
Love that is fire can burn, and were conscious of a
thirst, one only, one consuming thirst: Thou, O Lord,
art the Thing that I long for.

For what are all these glimpses, these unfoldings,
but the merest nothings in comparison with that for
which we wait?

> You meaner beauties of the night
> That poorly satisfy our sight,
> More by your number than your light;
>   You common people of the skies,
>   What are you when the moon shall rise?

Still, that starry hour was good, and in earlier
days the lover might have returned marked with the
Stigmata, a secret pain that would have throbbed in
unison with His, in foot and hand and side, while life
on earth did last, or so, indeed, it would have seemed
to one so fused in love with Him. But now our prayer

is rather for what the Stigmata signifies—"That I may know Him, and the power of His resurrection and the fellowship of His sufferings, being made conformable unto His death"—that is the sum of our prayer.

And yet something comes and draws Him very near when there is pain in a part of the body which He in His own Sacred Body gave to pain for us (though, indeed, no part was without urgent pain that day). I have told of how a verse in the poem *Stigmata* came close to me in the beginning. Now, as the year draws near to its end, another verse from the same poem carries another word:

> Must I be wounded in the busy hands
> That labour to fulfil
> Industrious love's demands
> Within the circle of Thy sovereign will?
> And can it fall within that will to let
> Thy child from all repayment of its debt?
> *Yea, this must be,*
> *If thou wouldst work for Me:*
> *Thus only can*
> *My seal be set on man.*

Those who have had that peculiarly piercing pain which is as though a nail were driven through the palm know how close it can draw the heart into a tender fellowship with Him whose two hands were pierced, not "as though," but in awful fact, by very nails of iron. There is a kind of solemn joy in coming in the flesh anywhere near the suffering flesh of our Lord. As a child I remember the thought of His

Divinity so far overwhelmed the thought of His humanity that it was impossible to realize that He suffered being tempted; and Calvary, though unspeakably awful, was so greatly overweighed by the thought of His spiritual pain that the physical passed a little out of sight. In a sense this is as it should be. The holy, pure, and beautiful spirit of our Saviour suffered so much more than we can understand that words fall off, afraid to touch so profound a mystery; but there was also the sensitive flesh born of a woman. There cannot be a pang in our flesh that was not, and sharper far, in that sacred Body on the Tree. And so in a new way, as we newly understand even only a little more of what He bore for us, we draw near to Him.

Sometimes in Dohnavur we, who dearly love the little children about us (and the older ones too), have looked up from some engrossing work to see a child beside us, waiting quietly. And when, with a welcoming hand held out, to the Tamil "I have come," we have asked "For what?" thinking, perhaps, of something to be confessed, or wanted, the answer has come back, "Just to love you." So do we come, Lord Jesus; we have no service to offer now; we do not come to ask for anything, not even for guidance. We come just to love Thee.

Not even for guidance. Three of our family were with me when the brier-bush story began. One drove off as quickly as Ford could go over a rough road to get help; another sat curled up uncomfortably, for what seemed a long time, trying to make me comfortable; and the third stood guard, gently but firmly persuading the friendly crowd of neighbors, each of whom had a pet remedy to recommend, to leave the twisted foot untouched. This gentle one has been my helper in preparing our rose for others; for the poor rose had to go into typescript, and when you are typing from penciled writing in a foreign language curious things may evolve. So as the pages were typed it was most helpful to have her go through them. She stopped at the words "not even for guidance." A typing slip? But no, they were what I had written. And I told her how for a time at least, till one could begin to serve a little again, there was no need to ask for guidance. The ill are the guided, not the guides. It had been a new experience; but the more you crush the leaves of the sweetbrier the more it offers its fragrance, and I had found, as I told her, unexpected sweetness in this new leaf. It is sometimes very good to ask nothing from our Lord, but to come "just to love Him."

There was a day in our Fellowship story when nothing seemed to matter, but only that in the grief which was upon us we should turn to Him. It was the day of this prayer-song:

> O Lord of Love and Lord of Pain,
>   Who by the bitter Cross
> Dost teach us how to measure gain,
>   And how to measure loss,
> Whom, seeing not, our hearts adore,
>   *We bring our love to Thee;*
> And where Thou art, Lord, evermore
>   Would we Thy servants be.

Will not those who are called to suffer let this comfort them? To them it is given to understand, more than ever before, of what Love has endured. In the pain, and very sensibly when it is over, and body, soul, and spirit lie back spent, there will be a sense of the clasping, the enfolding, of a love that passes knowledge. And though we can do nothing, the body being tied and bound, the spirit which no bonds can bind can bring its love to Him.

ONCE, being of a flute in need,
　　The Heavenly Shepherd sought
Until He found a bruisèd reed;
　　It was as if He thought
It precious; for aloud said He,
"This broken reed will do for Me."
It heard the kind word wonderingly,
　　Being a thing of naught.

And then that Lover of sweet sound,
　　No single note to lose,
Himself repaired the reed He found,
　　Well skilled such things to use.
This done, a happy melody
He whistled through it; "Now," said He,
"This flute of Mine shall stay by Me."
　　Thus He His flute did choose.

He said, "I play My country airs
　　The which do some displease;
But others, listening, find their cares
　　To pass, and sweet heartsease
Begin to blossom; and," said He
Unto His flute, "Thou, dear, with Me,
Wilt, making gentle minstrelsy,
　　Be comforter to these."

"Be comforter!" O bruisèd reed,
　　Dost seem a thing apart
From usual life of flowery mead?
　　What if, by His great art,
Perceiving what thou know'st not, He
Saith even now, "Yea, thou shalt be,
O broken reed, a flute for Me"?
　　O broken life, take heart.

24. AS BOUND WITH THEM

BUT to what end is pain? I do not clearly know. But I
have noticed that when one who has not suffered
draws near to one in pain there is rarely much power
to help; there is not the understanding that leaves the
suffering thing comforted, though perhaps not a
word was spoken; and I have wondered if it can be
the same in the sphere of prayer. Does pain accepted
and endured give some quality that would otherwise
be lacking in prayer? Does it create that sympathy
which can lay itself alongside the need, feeling it as
though it were personal, so that it is possible to do
just what the writer of Hebrews meant when he said,
"Remember them that are in bonds, *as bound with
them*; and them which suffer adversity, *as being your-
selves also in the body*"?

Most unforgettably we are also in the body. Often
I wonder how any doctor, knowing what doctors do
know, can have the heart to shut the door of the cage
when the bird is ready to fly out; but that is foolish-
ness, and I suppose, after all, most birds want to stay
in. However that may be, the fact remains that the
patients in the hospitals for incurables in every land,
and in all other hospitals and places where the suffer-

ing be, are very conscious of the body. Then here apparently is an opportunity. What if every stroke of pain, or hour of weariness, or loneliness, or any other trial of flesh or spirit, could carry us a pulse-beat nearer some other life, some life for which the ministry of prayer is needed, would it not be worth while to suffer? Ten thousand times yes. And surely it must be so, for the further we are drawn into the fellowship of Calvary with our dear Lord, the tenderer are we toward others, the closer alongside do our spirits lie with them that are in bonds; as being ourselves also in the body. God never wastes His children's pain.

A bruisèd reed shall He not break: the poorest shepherd boy on our South Indian hills is careful to choose,, for the making of his flute, a reed that is straight and fine and quite unbruised. But our Heavenly Shepherd often takes the broken and the bruised, and of such He makes His flutes. But life, like His book, is full of parables of tenderness; and one of these has often come into this room of late. For he whose name means God's Peace has brought his autoharp to play to me, and has first tuned it while I expectantly waited for the music which I knew would follow the tuning.

Is music to come from our harp? Music of prayer, of praise, of consolation? The strings are relaxed, or perhaps too tensely stretched. Illness can cause either condition. But we have a Tuner.

Tune Thou my harp;
There is not, Lord, could never be,
The skill in me.

Tune Thou my harp,
That it may play Thy melody,
Thy harmony.

Tune Thou my harp;
O Spirit, breathe Thy thought through me,
As pleaseth Thee.

NOTHING IN THE HOUSE

THY servant, Lord, hath nothing in the house,
Not even one small pot of common oil;
For he who never cometh but to spoil
Hath raided my poor house again, again,
That ruthless strong man armed, whom men call
    Pain.

I thought that I had courage in the house,
And patience to be quiet and endure,
And sometimes happy songs; now I am sure
Thy servant truly hath not anything,
And see, my songbird hath a broken wing.

*   *   *   *   *

My servant, I have come into the house—
I who know Pain's extremity so well
That there can never be the need to tell
His power to make the flesh and spirit quail:
Have I not felt the scourge, the thorn, the nail?

And I, his Conqueror, am in the house,
Let not your heart be troubled: do not fear:
Why shouldst thou, child of Mine, if I am here?
My touch will heal thy songbird's broken wing,
And he shall have a braver song to sing.

25. NOT ANYTHING IN THE HOUSE

I DO not think that we reach the place where we have "not anything in the house" until he whom men call Pain has raided us more than once or twice. The hardest days of the trouble that follows accident or illness are not the first days. They are the days later on, when a new assault of that strangely dreadful power finds us, as it were, at his feet defenseless.

On such days we are like the sailors of the psalm who do business in great waters: they mount up to the heaven, they go down again to the depths; their soul is melted because of trouble. And as the pretty songs of the Pippas of the earth ripple past us, we are only moved to a weary negation of their easy assertion. For though the lark's on the wing, the snail's on the thorn, and though well our hearts know that God's in His heaven, all's *not* right with the world. And we cannot "laugh in comforting of ourselves and joying in God for that the devil is overcome," for Apollyon appears to straddle quite over the whole breadth of the way, and swears we shall go no further; "here will I spill thy soul."

> Let nothing disturb thee,
> Nothing affright thee.

The words fly, like the lark on the wing, quite out of reach.

John Buchan's "Though I was afraid of many things, the thing I feared most mortally was being afraid," expresses us better. This cowardly intolerance of pain is the most disturbing thing that can be. To know that something must be borne or done, and to feel that one cannot stand it, is to be bereft of the last pot of oil. There is nothing to which a little more can be added; as in the story of the widow of Zarephath, there is just nothing. "Thy servant hath not anything in the house."

I who write have less cause to know this than many who will read. And yet I have known it. Where, then, were the promises on which I had lived all my life? Where was the triumphant "I can do all things through Christ which strengtheneth me"? Without these words that had never failed me all my life long I could only think of St. Paul's, "And when neither sun nor stars in many days appeared"; a few minutes without the sun and the familiar stars are like many days. It was at such a moment my dear nurse came into the room with something in her hands. It was a strip of teakwood carved with lotus, and between the lotus were these words:

> I will strengthen thee;
> Yea, I will help thee;
> Yea, I will uphold thee.

And she hung it where I could see it clearly.

The words were as familiar as the alphabet, but as

the whole beautiful verse, comfort of so many down the ages, came flowing over me—"Fear thou not; for I am with thee; be not dismayed; for I am thy God; I will strengthen thee; yea, I will help thee; yea, I will uphold thee with the right hand of My righteousness"—something happened. I looked, and I saw a pot of oil in the house.

But we have a God whose love is courageous. He trusts us to trust Him through the blind hours before we find our pot of oil, which indeed is always in the house. "Some of Love's secrets reveal others, and therefore between lovers there is recognition," so it is written in Ramón Lull's *Book of the Lover and the Beloved.* And it is one of the dearest secrets of love, that the lover can recognize as by some heavenly instinct the Presence of his Beloved, although he does not see Him. "Whom having not seen, ye love; in whom, though now ye see Him not, ye rejoice": thank God for the secrets of love.

IN SLEEP

He gives to His beloved in sleep,
For when the spirit drifts from fields of time,
And wanders free in worlds remote, sublime,
   It meets Him there,
   The only Alone Fair.
   But were it bidden to tell
   The heavenly words that fell,
Dropping like sunlit rain through quiet air,
It could not, though it heard them everywhere.

Were some small fish in rock-pool close confined,
Swept in the backwash of a wave to sea,
Could it describe that blue immensity?
   Could the caged bird,
   Whose happy ear had heard
   The lark sing in high heaven,
   And had escaped, be bidden
To bind that rapture fast in earthly words?
Not so is bound the song of singing birds.

Nor can I tell what He gave me in sleep—
The mind, still conscious of the body's stress,
Hindered awhile, and in a wilderness
   I walked alone,
   Till One a long time known
   Drew near; "Lord, may I come?
   For I would fain go Home."
"Not yet, My child," then waves on waves of blue.
Like the blue sea, or air that light pours through.

This is not much to bring of that land's gold.
But one word lingers of the shining dream,
"Be comforted, all ye who by a stream
   Watch wistfully,
   Lest your belovèd be
   Swept to some shore unknown,
   All desolate, alone;
It is not so, but now as heretofore,
The Risen Christ is standing on the shore."

26. IN SLEEP

THIS letter is for those who dearly love one who is ill, rather than for the ill. Between writing the last letter and beginning this, I have proved something to be true which I had believed before, but only because I believed those who told me of it. Now I know it in a different way.

Years ago, when Arulai Tara (whom some know as Star) was a young girl, she had enteric fever badly. One night when she was unconscious, a Hindu girl, Beauty, took refuge with us, and before dawn a clamorous crowd gathered round the house. Star was always much disturbed by noise, and, fearing for her in her weakness, I broke it to her gently when consciousness returned that there would be a noise which we could not stop, for a girl had come to us for refuge. "Beauty?" she said; "I spent last night with God for her." Then I knew that when the windows of the mind are closed the windows of the spirit may be open. And again when we were nursing Ponnamal, who was dying of cancer, several times, after what had appeared an extremity of distress, she told us that she herself had been in perfect peace with Christ all through those hours that to us seemed so dreadful.

But it is one thing to hear this and let it comfort you because you trust those who tell you about it, and quite another to know it yourself (even though in a much less degree) in such a way that you can say, "I know that it is so; *I have been there and found it so.*"

I am thinking now of you who watch by one whom you long to relieve and for whom you can do nothing. There is unconsciousness or semi-unconsciousness, and you cannot reach across the space between and touch that precious thing, the real person, the understanding soul. And yet, just here, you can help far more than you know. Long after power to speak or respond in any way has passed, that precious thing, dumb and blind and bound, but not deaf, and still quick in the body, can feel the handclasp and be strengthened by it, can hear and understand familiar words and be soothed and blessed by them. But there may be the added bitterness of pain, and when the reins of self-control have fallen from the fingers that would have held them to the end, if they could, there may be signs of that presence to the rending of your heart.

What word have I for you? Only this: The body may be held fast in misery, the mind may be wrestling with tyrannies it never met before—these things may be, but there is an end to them; they are only as a rough, short road to a great rest. Though to the traveler and to the watcher that road may not seem short, but more like a wild waste, a darkness with no end to it, there is an end. *After that ye have suffered awhile, But for a moment, If for a season,* are words of limitation very strong to succor. And suddenly, when

we come to the end, there is light. And though not a
glimmer of that light may fall on the watcher by the
bedside, the withdrawn spirit is bathed in radiant
waves. As a fish in the sea, as a bird in the air, so is that
spirit free, so is it gay. For it is not where it seems to
be, but otherwhere. Our Lord has met it. He is
speaking now, "Be of good cheer: it is I; be not
afraid." There may be nothing to tell the watcher
anything of this, and yet it is neither myth nor mirage,
but truth: I have proved it true.

The words that face this letter came before the
memory of an experience new to me had fallen back
into the mist. That memory is misty now. I could not,
however much I tried, recover a line of this that tells
what it can of those hours. It was to a mind still half
asleep those words came. And as they whispered
through that half-sleep, a wondering question came
with them: *From thy brier shall blow a rose for
others*—could this be that? So they were dictated
slowly in that parched hour, between teaspoonfuls of
water (I remember thinking that a whole glassful at a
time would be pure bliss), and the faithful little
night-nurse by the bedside wrote them down. But
whether there be anything here that can be called a
rose or not, this other, this heavenly rose of comfort,
cannot fail: Underneath them—your beloved—are
the everlasting arms. They are safe there. Let not
your heart be troubled, you who care so much. He
cares still more. He *cannot* fail the child who trusts
Him. Heaven and earth may fail; He cannot. God is
our refuge and strength, a very present help in trouble. (Is not *this* trouble?) Therefore will not we fear,

though the earth be removed, and though the mountains be carried into the midst of the sea; though the waters thereof roar and be troubled, though the mountains shake with the swelling thereof. God is in the midst of her (that heart you love so well); she shall not be moved: God shall help her, and that right early.

Let these strong words uphold you; they are being fulfilled now in the secret cell of the spirit of that lover of the Lord. However things may be with the body and the mind, however they may appear to be, let not your heart be troubled, neither let it be afraid.

And should you have to face an operation for one you love, here is a word which may help. We of this household have lately proved its strength and sweetness for two of our members, one English and one Indian, who have just been through major operations. It was the verse given to their nurse on the morning of the operation, "When the doors were shut came Jesus and stood in the midst, and saith unto them, Peace be unto you." The doors of a hospital theater are not shut for fear of the Jews; even so it is a perfect word, for in the place of the shut door there is He as of old, and He says to His own to-day, just as He did long ago, *Peace be unto you.*

But if they go from you, those whom you so desire to keep, and the sense of silence and of absence settles down upon you, aches through you and will not cease, and the accustomed platitudes of comfort are torn like veils in the wind—the wild craving of the heart bereft can be like a raging wind—perhaps this quiet word from a quiet book will help:

The Lord give you great and holy liberty in intercourse with Him about your Dorothy. Oh, how He understands our hearts! I dare not limit what your Lord may permit you of insight into your darling's present personal bliss and intense spiritual nearness to you and union with you. To some the Lord grants what can only be called visions. We have never had one, only one or two deeply sweet dreams: one in which her dear face turned suddenly on me with an extraordinarily radiant look of bliss in herself and love to me.

But we honour the Lord most by simply living on His Word about them and us, and growing into *that*.

"Ye are *come unto* the spirits of the just made perfect." That is close neighbourhood.*

His Word soon brings us to the Cloud of witnesses who compass us about.† Would the thought of that shining Cloud, that dense mass of living, loving beings encircling us, be used to help our patience if it were not true that the heavenly watchers care about each several runner on the racecourse of the earth, and that our beloved remember? (How could they forget?) Sometimes the comfort that is there is dimmed by the fear that if they see good and are glad, they may see ill and grieve. But that fear is answered by all that we know of the hereafter. The two companions of immortals who talked with our Lord Jesus about His Passion did not say, Pity Thyself. They understood. They could bear to look at Calvary. They had seen what lay beyond.

* *Bishop Handley Moule*, Harford and Macdonald.

† A cloud is used in all languages for a dense mass of living beings, from the time of Homer downwards (Westcott).

But there are some among us whose heartbreak is that they have no sure and certain hope about their dearest, who have passed beyond reach of human love and influence. May I offer this which comes to me in the form of a question: Does to be out of reach of our love and influence mean to be out of reach of His who said, "I, if I be lifted up from the earth, will draw all men unto Me"?

LOVER Divine, whose love has sought and found me,
Thou dost not leave me when the night is round me;
Cause me to be, held fast by Love eternal,
More than a conqueror.

Open mine eyes to see the stars above me,
Quicken my heart that I may feel Thee love me,
Make me, and keep me through Thy love eternal,
More than a conqueror.

What storm can shatter, gloom of darkness frighten
One whom the Lord doth shelter, cherish, lighten?
O let me be, through powers of love eternal,
More than a conqueror.

Therefore He saith thus: *Pray inwardly, though thee thinketh it savour thee not: for it is profitable, though thou feel not, though thou see nought; yea, though thou think thou canst not. For in dryness and in barrenness, in sickness and in feebleness, then is thy prayer well-pleasant to Me, though thee thinketh it savour thee nought but little. And so is all thy believing prayer in My sight . . . .*God accepteth the good-will and the travail of His servant, howsoever we feel.

JULIAN OF NORWICH.

27. TEMPTATION IN ILLNESS

"ALL the little shades of feeling which make the common fine," the difficult easy, the depressing glad, have been about me from the first day until now, and yet, with so little reason for temptation, there are days when I have to say to myself,

> Be triumphant, be triumphant,
> *Let the spiritual watchers see*
> *That thy God doth strengthen thee,*
> *That in Him is victory,*

and the words "Pharaoh, King of Egypt, is but a noise" are often a great solace. But I felt that there must be temptations which I had not met, even though, having nursed my Indian children, I did know something of what illness could do. So I asked my dear nurse what in her experience were the chief trials of the ill. "Oh, there are many. There is monotony: the same ward, the same routine, the same food, the same faces, the same sounds, the same pain if it is chronic trouble. Life in an incurable hospital can be terribly monotonous. And there is weariness and loneliness and despondency, and the temptation to feel neglected and forgotten, and that no one knows how bad the pain is, perhaps that no one cares. And there is the fear of pain. After long suffering this fear can be very hard to bear." How well I knew the truth of that last word. "Through constant watchings wise," I thought as I listened, and I thought, too, how much a nurse's eyes see, and I felt how very unsuitable it was for one who has felt so few of these things to write to those who are caught in that thorny thicket. It should be a nurse who writes. A nurse knows more than anyone else of what illness (and even convalescence) can mean of strain to body and to spirit, and how unlike the wise man of the *Imitation* the ill and tired may be. He, being well-taught in spirit, standeth, "taking none heed what he feel in himself, nor on which side the wind of unstableness bloweth." We are not like that. Nor are we like the true lover whose love beareth evenly every uneven thing. But Rotherham's translation of Job 24: 12, comforter of low moments, comes to mind: "The soul of the wounded calleth for help, and God doth not regard it as foolish." Whatever the wounding be, however trivial it may appear, so that the soul would be ashamed to tell its inward distress, from whatever side the wind of unstableness bloweth, the soul of the wounded may call for help, and God will not regard it as foolish. Quick upon the call will come deliverance. Something will occur to break the monotony—if nothing outward, then something inward. Some little candle will be lit; the dull fog will lift; it must be so. "My hand was stretched out in the night, and slacked not." "God is mine illumination and mine health.

Whom shall I dread?" "I am in a manner imprisoned and grievously fettered till" (blessed *till*) "Thou refresh me with the light of Thy presence." And then? But who can tell it? Who can tell what Thou art, O Lord? Who can tell what Thou doest? Who can show to another what Thy large grace can be?

Pain cannot shut the door to Thee, nor fatigue refuse Thee, nor languor dim the clear shining of Thy face. I could not by searching find the peace that Thou givest. The depth saith, It is not in me; and the sea saith, It is not with me. It cannot be gotten for gold, neither shall silver be weighed for the price thereof, and the exchange of it shall not be for jewels of fine gold. But Thy word abideth for ever: "Peace I leave with you, My peace I give unto you; not as the world giveth, give I unto you. Let not your heart be troubled, neither let it be afraid."

O LORD, we bring Thee him for whom we pray,
Be Thou his strength, his courage, and his stay,
And should his faith flag as he runs the race,
Show him again the vision of Thy face.

Be Thou his vision, Lord of Calvary,
Hold him to follow, hold him fast by Thee
O Thou who art more near to us than air,
Let him not miss Thee, ever, anywhere.

28. THE OX-GOAD OF SHAMGAR

IT is evening. I am alone except for a disconsolate Lotus (we have such at times) who has settled down beside me to read to herself. The room is lighted and cheery. Outside it is dark, with a monsoon feel in the air (it is late October now), and the damp dark seems to be trying to get in through the four open windows and two open doors. But it cannot get in, and the light shines on a great beautiful mass of color on a small table; green and rose caladium leaves, large caladium flowers with spathes like white wings round the pale golden pillar of the spadix; and fern, a running root of it over two feet long, with wonderful brown and green oak-leaf fronds—a treasure from the forest; for all the dear people who went there brought down of its treasures to make my room foresty. The family is engaged with itself, brothers English and Indian with boys and men, and sisters with women and girls and babies, doctors and nurses with the sick in our home hospital and the Door of Health (an Indian house used while the hospital, Place of Spiritual Healing, as it is called, is being built). And I had counted on an empty hour, when the nurse of nurses came in. Attending her, like a devoted acolyte, was the young

Suseela (the salaaming baby of *Lotus Buds,* page 116), bearing a familiar tray with dressings.

It is most interesting to see one's children handling surgical mysteries, and while the nurse of nurses washed her hands with the usual almost religious ritual, I watched this Lotus Bud with her tray of untouchables, and thought many thoughts that do not belong to roses from briers and so shall be un-written; only, because these letters will go to some who have helped to bring these things to pass, helped to draw from the pit of corruption these Lotus Bud children, helped to create this family of between five and six hundred, with its outposts and its far-flowing influences, there must be this one word, Thank you, friends of our Lord, and of the children.

The ritual of the hand-washing and subsequent ministrations over, it was too late to write, and now in the intervals of a full day, for many matters come to this happy room, I am thinking of other temptations. "Disease produces much selfishness. A man in pain is looking after ease; and lets most other things go as chance shall dispose of them," wrote Samuel Johnson out of the dejection of long illness. The trial of help-lessness can turn to fierce irritation for one accus-tomed to paddling his own canoe, and the inability to do anything with vigor, perhaps unexpected out-crops of weakness, can cause convalescence to be an unpeaceful time. But for all this, He who is our strength, our peace, our patience, can suffice. A single promise upon which the soul fastens, and to which it clings for very life, can open the doors of the deepest dungeon of the prison-house, even that prison-house of which I told in the letter called "Not Anything in the House." To be unable to say with the courageous Samuel, "The pain I hope to endure with decency," is to be there. When he said that, he was facing the amputation of his foot without an anesthetic. What is your pin-prick compared with that? you ask yourself, but you cannot taunt yourself out of a dungeon; you only pile up dungeon-feelings; for the thought of another's distress, even though it be long past, doubles your own. But the old story is true: "I have a key in my bosom, called *Promise,* that will, I am persuaded, open any lock. Then said Hopeful, That's good news; good brother, pluck it out of thy bosom and try."

There was a day when the fear of breaking under more pain was such that I was on the point of destroying these letters, because to fail there would be to prove them indeed the merest paper-grace. A few nights later, after the key had opened that lock, one of the Psalms for the evening said: "If the Lord had not helped me, it had not failed but my soul had been put to silence." I understood that word then as I never had before.

It is strange how as one walks down any new road it opens on either side into dim, unexplored avenues. One such has opened during these months. I had thought of patients in hospitals as certainly relieved from pain by one or other of the wonderful means now known to science. I had seen the quick relief given to patients in our little hospital after operation, and had thought that this good help was possible in any illness. I have learned that often it cannot be given. There is pain that cannot rightly be relieved. It may bite and gnaw like a living tooth, but so long as it bites and gnaws only the edges of being, that tooth must work its will. Never before have I understood how near to such a state is the foul temptation of cowardice. To feel like saying to that tooth, "Go deeper and have done with it," is cowardice; but there it is. Perhaps if the well should chance on this page, to look down this unexplored avenue might lead to a new understanding, and so to a new power to help those to whom is appointed pain that passes allowable means of relief, and yet is not fatal to life, and so cannot be stilled. Often just to understand is to help.

And now I hesitate to write what is so absurdly small that the strong in soul will smile, and yet Shamgar the son of Anath slew six hundred men with an ox-goad. An ox-goad is a stick with a nail in its tip—a mere stick.

There is something as insignificant that can slay that without which we perish spiritually—our tranquillity. To awaken after a dream of health, and find that it was only a dream, is to feel the prick of the ox-goad of Shamgar, and a pricked soul is not tranquil. The blind has seen beloved faces and all beautiful things, and could read; the deaf has heard voices and laughter, music and the wind in the trees, singing birds and the sound of flowing water; the maimed has run a race and won; the child has been home again; the mother has been with her children. A vivid moment of freedom, delight, health, timeless as dream-moments are, the filling up to overflowing of the cup of heart's desire, then a sudden or a gradual coming back to reality—a prick, a score of pricks, feelings that prick sharply: who can fight feelings so small but so devastating?

There is One who can, and to Him we may turn with a word that He Himself gives us to say: *Fight against them that fight against me.* Does the maker forget that of which his handiwork is made? He remembers that we are dust. To Him nothing is insignificant, not even the pricks of an ox-goad. Feelings are not too small for His loving regard.

Among the temptations of illness is one which I omitted—the lack of privacy. It can be an ox-goad. When you cannot any more shut your door, cannot count on being alone, it is easy to forget that there is another door which can be shut. We can sink deep into the quietness which is within and not without, and so is not affected by that which is without. We can emerge (as it were) from that stillness at a word, at a touch, and yet remain within it. In Him, not in our circumstances, is our peace. As of old, it is today. In Christ, in Colosse; in Christ, in hospital; in Christ, *here.*

> O Thou who are more near to us than air,
> Let me not miss Thee, ever, anywhere.

LORD, art Thou wrapped in cloud,
    That prayer should not pass through?
But heart that knows Thee sings aloud,
    Beyond the grey, the blue;
Look up, look up to the hills afar,
And see in clearness the Evening Star.

Should misty weather try
    The temper of the soul,
Come, Lord, and purge and fortify,
    And let Thy hands make whole,
Till we look up to the hills afar,
And see in clearness the Evening Star.

Oh, never twilight dim
    But candles bright are lit,
And then the heavenly vesper hymn—
    The peace of God in it,
As we look up to the hills afar,
And see in clearness the Evening Star.

29. SECOND CAUSES—PERSIAN CARPETS

IN a letter of Samuel Rutherford's dated 1640, he speaks about the difficulty of being patient if we stay our thoughts "down among the confused rollings and wheels of second causes, as, Oh the place! Oh the time! Oh if this had not been, this had not followed! Oh the linking of this accident with this time and place! Look up to the master-motion and the first wheel."

If this had not been, this had not followed—how exactly true to life. The temptation to think along these lines can be vinegar upon niter. That day, now over a year ago, when we four happy people found the little low door leading into the courtyard of the house we had rented in Joyous City locked, we stood outside wondering what we should do. The old man who had charge of the key was not there, and the key was not to be found.

So we stood in the swiftly gathering twilight, ready to turn contentedly and go home if we could not get in. Just then another old man hurried up, the huge key of his own courtyard door in his hands. "This may open it," he said hopefully; there was a minute's fumbling, the door opened, and we went in. If the old man had not hurried up with a key? If the door had not opened? The confused rollings and wheels of second causes do not help us much here, or anywhere. The Lord allowed it. Therefore, so far as we are concerned, He did it. Himself hath done it. And all He does is good. And what a special kindness to allow a disablement to come in the direct line of duty—we thank Thee, O Father.

There is another word in Rutherford's Letters which often helps: "They who contend with Zion see not what He is doing when they are set to work, as undersmiths or servants, to the work of refining the saints. Satan's hand also, by them, is at the melting of the Lord's vessels of mercy, and their office in God's house is to scour and cleanse vessels for the King's table."

The coolies who dug the pit where no pit was supposed to be, the old man who did not leave the key in its right place and so caused delay till dusk turned to dark, were the undersmiths, and all the troubles that followed were only scullions cleansing and scouring together for good.

But there are limits set to the activities of the smiths and the scullions. On October 6 a member of our Fellowship who was in prayer in London was suddenly caused to feel that danger was threatening the one here who, eighteen days afterwards, fell into that pit in the dark. He prayed, not the easy prayer of the unconcerned, but the prayer of the greatly burdened. There was a sense of fear upon him, as of a terror by night. Then peace came, and he knew that his prayer was heard. And these who have tended the months know that such a fall might have been far more serious in its effect. The least, not the greatest, harm it could have done was allowed. But that was not all. Four or five hours later, as the motor lorry with its cargo of the whole and maimed was on its way to Neyyoor in the black night, in torrents of rain on a flooded road built up between rice fields and water, it crossed a deep fissure caused by the washing away of part of the road, where a tree had been torn up by the roots and flung down the steep bank.

The lorry was going at such speed that it had no time to sink into the hole; all of us were for a moment tossed like balls, and the injured limb in its splints, jerked out of the hand that held it, came down on the lorry floor with a thud. These rifts are often of unknown depth and extent and can be dangerous. Only the angels, and the Lord of the angels, who had set a skilled hand at the wheel, saved it from plunging into the rice field, just then a swamp, or the deep water on the other side. If the lorry had gone over either unprotected edge it would almost certainly have turned as it fell, and we should have been drowned or smothered in mud.

But it did not go over the edge. And yet if it had? Should we have said that prayer was not answered? It is a petty view of our Father's love and wisdom which demands or expects an answer according to our desires, apart from His wisdom. We see hardly one inch of the narrow lane of time. To our God eternity lies open as a meadow. It must seem strange to the heavenly people who have seen the beautiful End of the Lord, that we should ever question what Love allows to be, or ever call a prayer "unanswered" when the answer is not what we expect; as one of our baby songs says, "Isn't *No* an answer?" And where what is called a fatal accident is concerned I feel like adding, "Isn't heaven an answer?"

LORD, Thou hast suffered, Thou dost know
The thrust of pain, the piercing dart,
How wearily the wind can blow
Upon the tired heart.

He whom Thou lovest, Lord, is ill.
O come, Thou mighty Vanquisher
Of wind and wave, say, Peace, be still,
Eternal Comforter.

Defend and keep the soul of Thy little servant among so
many perils of this corruptible life, and Thy grace going
with him, direct him by the way of peace to the country of
everlasting brightness. Amen, Amen.

The Imitation (Close of the third book of
Inward Consolation).

O Christian worker, Christian soldier, Christian pilgrim, in the midst of your "contest" and your "running"
to-day, or in what *seems* the midst of it, for the end may all
the while be just upon you, take heart often from the
thought that even so for you, if you are true to the blessed
Name, it shall one day be. The last care will have been felt,
and cast upon the Lord, the last exhausting effort will have
been made, the last witness under difficulties borne, the
last sorrow faced and entered, the last word written, the
last word spoken. And then the one remaining thing will
be to let the Lord, "the Man at the Gate," lift thee in, and
give thee rest.

BISHOP MOULE on 2 Timothy 4: 7.

30. THE LONG LANE

THE beautiful paragraph closing with the Man at the Gate lifting us in, giving us rest, must have been to multitudes a very word from heaven. It has been with me ever since I read it first in the heat of battle in 1906.

And so I believe that the way of peace is found in looking on to the End of the Lord, not in puzzling over the beginning or the middle of His ways. The brother who drove us that night through the rain along the dark road had been to Persia. He told us how the famous carpets are made by two sets of workers working towards the center. They sit on a bench on one side of the warp, which is hung from a beam above. The designer stands on the other. He holds the pattern in his hand and directs the workers by calling across to them, in a kind of chant, exactly what they are to do. Near them are variously colored bobbins; they chant back to him the word that they have heard, cut from the appointed bobbin a length of thread, push it through the suspended warp and knot it. They see nothing of the pattern till the carpet is finished. Then the designer cuts off the loose threads and shears the pile down to the required level. The workers choose nothing, see nothing. Their responsibility is simply to listen and obey.

But when the carpet is finished, the blending of color with color is seen, and how each several knotted thread had its part to play in the design.

We are now in November 1932, and a letter has come today from one who is more in bonds than I am, though she can walk about. There is a sentence in her letter that brings her straight into our company.

She speaks of "the long spell of pain which seems to be far from being over even now, though it is more than five weeks since the operation," and tells how she has gone daily to the hospital for the last three weeks for treatment. "And that may have to continue for a long time."*

What you say about such times being opportunities of proving His promises and finding a little bit at a time to be spirit and life has been exactly my experience. Sometimes when I have had to go through a painful dressing, or the reopening of a wound that was closing too quickly, the only thing has been first to drop into His arms and put upon Him the whole responsibility of making His word a reality. I have longed that it might be made real to others also through this. I like the translation of Rotherham that you sent, so much (Psalm 63: 8: "My soul hath run clinging to Thee, on me hath Thy right hand laid hold"). The thought in it has often come to me these days. I have been too weak to cling sometimes, so He has had to grasp me. Surely of all places

---

*The "long time" was shortened. She passed out of reach of pain a few weeks later.

where His presence is a reality the bed of pain is especially so. We do know that these light afflictions (which sometimes seem very heavy) are working for us a far more exceeding and eternal weight of glory. How marvelous the contrast! Surely in the contemplation of it we can begin to praise in the furnace.

I have copied this partly for the sake of the well, who may perhaps chance upon these letters. It is easy to think the worst is over when an operation is over. It was done under a general anesthetic—there was not even the nervous tension of a local; and we think (when we are well) of a few days' discomfort, and forget how long and wretched the nights that belong to and follow those days may be, for not all nights can be soothed by opiates. And we forget or give only a passing thought to the after-treatment that sometimes (though not always, thank God), coming on top of all that went before, may be a very trying thing for one already tired out with pain.

I want to touch as many of the strings of the harp of pain as I can, and so I am moved to emphasize the usually forgotten, and to ask the better and the well to help the ill through what may be the hardest part of all, if the trouble be like a very long lane with no turning even in sight. Help them through by not forgetting how long and how rough to the feet that lane can be. "He comforteth them that are losing patience" is a sweet little word from Ecclesiasticus. He does indeed, and He calls for fellow-comforters.

AUTUMN

O GIVER of my lovely green in spring,
　A dancing, singing green upon my tree,
My green has passed; I have no song to sing,
　What will my autumn be?

Must it be, though alive, as all but dead,
　A heavy-footed and a silent thing?
Effectless, sapless, tedious, limited,
　A withered vanishing?

*　　　*　　　*　　　*　　　*

Thus I. But He to me: Have I not shown
　In glowing woodland's golden parable
The splendour of My purpose for Mine own,
　I, their Immanuel?

Now shalt thou see, My child, what I will do;
　For as thy lingering autumn days unfold,
The lovely singing green of hitherto
　Will come to thee in gold.

31. AT A GREAT DISTANCE

THERE has no temptation taken you but such as is common to man, so this which I will copy from a friend's letter will speak perhaps to many. It spoke to me because, as I wrote before, I had not thought of any autumn. I had prayed and confidently expected a quick flight on a midsummer day. But a tree in autumn foliage is not a painted fraud, nor is the word of the living God of none effect.

> The devil was tempting me the other day in a time of much physical weakness and some loneliness of spirit, by suggesting that God did not seem to be keeping His promise about something long prayed for. I picked up a large-type R.V. New Testament which I generally read in bed, opened it at random, and these words stood out on the page. *But it is not as though the word of God hath come to nought.* And in a flash I saw afresh that the Lord has wider purposes and something bigger for us than we think, that we must not miss the greater by fixing our whole attention on the less. He that believeth on Him shall not be put to shame

But the soul of the ill is a curious thing; it may settle on some rock of assurance, and then be swept off its feet by a new wave, just when it had begun to look forward to the blessing of quietness, just when it was learning to say contentedly, "All the days of my appointed time will I wait till my change come." Even its nearest hardly understand if it foolishly tells of this private wave. But lately a friend expressed it unconsciously and perfectly as she spoke of an invalid so tenderly sheltered "that she is likely to live for years." It sounded as though she meant that the angel of death could hardly find his way into a room whose doors and windows were so carefully shut against him. Yes, that is it; that is the heart's unspoken fear, and with the word the enemy comes in like a flood. Is *this* room so protected that he will not be able to find the way in for a long, long time? "Though our outward man perish, yet the inward man is renewed day by day"; like the white wings of flying birds against a dark cloud, so are such words as they glance across the troubled mind; but how can the outward perish if loving hands take such care of it? To live in vigor —we are ready for that, however many be the years appointed; to be folded up in the soft wrappings of luxurious ease—that is different.

But anything that brings to memory the vision of St. John, "His servants shall serve Him and they shall see His face," or St. Paul's, "The Lord Himself shall descend from heaven with a shout," can call those floods of longing. The tale of one whose warfare is accomplished, perhaps after a very short fight, the enchantment of music, the cadence of a hymn, can call them. The kindling words, "Oh, think, to clasp a hand outstretched, and that God's hand; to breathe new air, and that celestial air; to feel refreshed, and know it immortality. Oh, think, to pass from storm and stress to one unbroken calm, to wake and find it glory," can carry us up to the "top of the house" and show us what the pilgrim saw: "And behold at a great distance, he saw a most pleasant mountainous country, beautified with woods, vineyards, fruits of all sorts, flowers also, with springs and fountains, very delectable to behold. Then he asked the name of the country. They said it was Immanuel's Land." And then we have to go downstairs again; the land is at a great distance; farther away than even that which the pilgrims saw later from the hill called *Clear,* when, looking through the glass, they thought they saw something like the Gate, and also some of the glory of the place—and the enemy comes in like a flood.

Is there no standard to lift up against him? Must we be perpetually enfeebled by homesickness of the heart? "When the enemy shall come in like a flood, the Spirit of the Lord shall lift up a standard against him"—there we have it. As the sight of a triumphant flag to a smitten foe, so is the word of the Lord our Deliverer to him who would shatter our peace. We need not be overwhelmed.

How foolish this letter will appear to the well and the able, who have only to will and do. But I hope that they will not read it. It is not for them. It is only for those whom pain has sorely tried and who are discovering how intricate is the intertwining of spirit, soul, and body. Arguments, expostulations, sensible reflections, good advice, have no effect upon that entangled fact.

But this does not excuse weakness, nothing does, and the wise old Rutherford has often shamed me: "I wonder many times that a child of God should ever have a sad heart, considering what their Lord is preparing." "I go to prepare a place for you. I will come again and receive you unto Myself." "Home unto Myself "—oh word of infinite peace!

Today my golden picture of horse chestnuts in autumn was set in front of me. And I let it speak to me as it never fails to speak. To the young who come into my room it is just a beautiful picture. Their autumn is far out of sight; but I offer its luminous word to all to whom it has a voice. What does "the inward man is renewed day by day" mean if it does not mean that our God will give gold for green, spiritual vigor, the shining heart that can be content and more than content, *delighted* with whatever His will may prove to be till He comes again to receive us unto Himself? Such victory of spirit over flesh is miracle, but we learn to expect miracles from the God who can turn the green of spring to gold.

THY JOHN

As John upon his dear Lord's breast,
So would I lean, so would I rest;
As empty shell in depths of sea,
So would I sink, be filled with Thee.

As water-lily in her pool
Through long, hot hours is still and cool,
A thought of peace, so I would be
Thy water-flower, Lord, close by Thee.

As singing bird in high, blue air,
So would I soar, and sing Thee there;
Nor rain, nor stormy wind can be
When all the air is full of Thee.

And so though daily duties crowd,
And dust of earth be like a cloud,
Through noise of words, O Lord, my Rest,
Thy John would lean upon Thy breast.

32. LEARNING TO DO WITHOUT

"Do they ever get accustomed to being ill?" I once asked about some whose trials lay heavy upon me. I was told that they did. I doubt it now. The doctor may get accustomed to seeing them so, the nurse to looking after them, the visitor to bringing them flowers, other people to thinking of them, but do they ever wake up in the morning without the longing of a caged bird to fly? Do they ever grow accustomed to the weariness of helplessness? to the *not* being able? to broken nights? to lack of ease? to pain? I think that others may grow accustomed to the thought of this for them. I doubt if they ever grow accustomed to it for themselves. But leaving aside the greater tribulation of the incurable, there is the long illness, the delayed recovery, the unfitness where fitness was so keenly expected that in imagination it had all but come. Does anyone (always excepting the nurse if she be understanding) see anything of this? If things are beautifully managed, all that is apparent is that unburdened tranquillity which looks so restful, and the gentle comforts of love abounding. No one sees the hidden bird beating its wings. No one, thank God, can feel the weary waking in the morning, the longing that comes just to be out of pain.

"Surely I have behaved and quieted myself, as a child that is weaned of his mother; my soul is even as a weaned child." It is the word for one "who is learning to do without"—without health, without power to go about like others, do things, enjoy things, be in the joyful stream of things, and, for many, much more than this.

I have written elsewhere a sentence from a letter Bishop Moule wrote to me after he was bereaved of what he called "the darling love" of wife and child, but it has helped so many that I will write it again: *I am learning the lesson set to the weaned child; I am learning to do without.*

And after writing a foreword to the story of Ponnamal, a dear Indian sister, he wrote from the depths of his own experience:

Ah, we need a Saviour perfectly versed in every anguish of the heart when we are called to great personal losses, to give up for ever on earth the face and voice and intercourse of our Ponnamals. But He entirely understands, and He will come again with them. May your beloved Lord's presence be more and yet more consciously surrounding and fulfilling. In a wonderful way He can fill (not close) the wounds of love, making each a receptacle for Himself:

Thy Jesus can repay
From His own fullness all He takes away.

There is only one place where we can receive the

gift of a great contentment in such a doing without. The last verse of the little song that faces this letter is thinking of the normal day when duties that seem to jostle one another (though, properly understood, duties never do jostle) crowd all round us. We have known that day. How good it would be to feel its careless touch again. But even for us who are guarded from it, whether for months or years, there can be a crowding of thoughts, even perhaps a noise of words, a dust of earth that can utterly banish the sweetness of His felt presence. But it need not be so. We are all Thy Johns, Lord Jesus. Thy John would lean upon Thy breast.

Do we not hear Thy footfall, O Belovèd,
 Among the stars on many a moonless night?
Do we not catch the whisper of Thy coming
 On winds of dawn, and often in the light
Of noontide and of sunset almost see Thee?
 Look up through shining air
And long to see Thee, O Belovèd, long to see Thee,
 And wonder that Thou art not standing there?

And we shall hear Thy footfall, O Belovèd,
 And starry ways will open, and the night
Will call her candles from their distant stations,
 And winds shall sing Thee, noon, and mingled
  light
Of rose-red evening thrill with lovely welcome;
 And we, caught up in air,
Shall see Thee, O Belovèd, we shall see Thee,
 In hush of adoration see Thee there.

33. AS WE HAVE BORNE

In *The Spirit of Discipline* Bishop Paget has a chapter called "The Hope of the Body." This is a sentence from it:

> There is a deep and wonderful prophecy in that inscrutable interaction of soul and body which may sometimes startle, or bewilder, or distress us; it hints at the hope of the body, the opportunity of the soul; it means that the body also is accessible to the Divine life; that there are avenues by which the power of the Resurrection can invade it; that it is capable of a transfiguration; that for it too the Lord from heaven is a quickening Spirit.

And he speaks of our very bodies being affected by a real energy from the indwelling of the Spirit of Christ, so that the power of His resurrection may extend even to the physical conditions of our life,

> . . . that very slowly and partially, it may be, with limits that are soon reached, and hindrances that will not yield, yet, for all that, very truly and practically, the redemption of our body may be begun on earth.

Is not all this full of vital things for us who are ill or in any kind of bonds? Here am I, here are you, in an ordinary bed, or an ordinary chair, very conscious of the earthliness of this body of our humiliation, as St. Paul so extremely truthfully calls it, and we cannot get away from it. It will not let us, as we gladly would, forget it.

But "*As we have borne* the image of the earthy, *we shall also bear* the image of the heavenly," is not the only word of comfort that God has for us; He has this other, this that deals with our today (as that does with our tomorrow) in such a glorious happy way that we are ashamed that we ever, even if but for one minute, fail to rise to its bright beckoning: "There are avenues by which the power of the Resurrection can invade it now; it is capable of transfiguration."

Lord, transfigure it; this dust, enlighten it; cause Thy life to flow that it may "not be brought under the power of the things that so often domineer," but even now be prepared for the time when "it will be wholly penetrated and transfigured by the spirit of the Lord."

And till that good time comes? There is one thing we can always do. We can find the incense trees that grow in our hottest places. We can offer Him our hearts' adoration.

Among the joys of these months have been the books sent by friends who understand what escape from pain can be found in a book. The first of this company of book-friends was the gallant and beautiful Lady Victoria Buxton. She found her incense trees.

She was struck down suddenly, a lovely young wife and mother, in February 1869, and held fast by "searching and exhausting pain" till July 1916. Forty-seven years of pain. And yet her life was one of valorous patience, forgetfulness of self, service to others; and such a sense of light was about her that after she had passed a daughter could write:

> Was she helpless, always in pain, bound wearily to couch and chair? If it was so, it is not suffering and sadness that speak of her. Rather it is the beauty of sunshine and roses, the shimmer on the river, the blue haze on the summer sea. These things speak of her, not those others.

And a friend wrote:

> An hour spent in her quiet sitting-room was enough to give one an entirely new view of illness and its possibilities. There were, indeed, the outward signs of an invalid's condition—the "prone-couch," the sofa, the walking-sticks always at hand, the little meal brought in on a tray at 5 o'clock. There were visible in the worn face and attenuated frame—even more touchingly in the fading eyes—the unmistakable evidences of long-continued suffering. But all this was only, as it were, the setting of the picture—the central figure was a spiritual presence, which bodily pain and lassitude were powerless to affect.

But hers was not a cheaply won victory of spirit over flesh. This is from her private papers:

> Things do *not* improve, and use is *not* a "second na-

ture," and all seems increasingly hard sometimes, and I am rather hopeless of getting better. . . . What should I do without Him, in life or death? The inner loneliness would be awful, in spite of all that human affection could do for me. We need a friend, above all a Saviour, in the depths of our being—and, thank God, we have one.

And so she loved, served, shone, was more than conqueror. And fortified and comforted for those forty-seven years, a very St. John in her day and generation, she gave to all who saw her an entirely new view of sickness and its possibilities.

LORD, more and more
I pray Thee, or by wind or fire,
Make pure my inmost heart's desire,
And purge the clinging chaff from off the floor.

I wish Thy way,
But when in me myself would rise
And long for something otherwise,
Then, Holy One, take sword and spear, and slay.

Oh, stay near by,
Most patient Love, till, by Thy grace,
In this poor silver, Thy bright face
Shows forth in clearness and serenity.

What will it be
When, like the lily or the rose
That in my flowery garden blows,
I shall be flawless, perfect, Lord, to Thee?

34. CHRYSALIDES

A FEW days ago one of the children strung sixteen chrysalides on a thread of raffia and sent the pretty necklet to me. It was hung where I could see it, and this morning by each of the empty colorless shells, which yesterday were silver caskets, sat a butterfly drying its wings. Presently the happy things fluttered off and lighted on a Lotus Bud who stood near, and from her they flew to me, too young in the new life of liberty to know a fear, then, quick with the rapture of freedom, they flew out into the sunshine.

I am told that even though life can only mean more suffering, most people want to go on living. (I think they are very brave.) But there are times when we are rent by desire for the liberty of wings. And words nearly five hundred years old come to mind: "Behold my soul, shut in my body's jail." Thoughts turn wistfully then to our Lord's "It is finished"; the very words breathe rest.

This surge of longing that pushes up from time to time may become such a sharp and recurring temptation that I revert to it again. Before that word of peace was spoken on the Cross, our Lord, in the midst of the heat and the toils of the day, had said:

"My meat is to do the will of Him that sent Me, and to finish His work." I think we do well to take this handful of snow and lay it on our heart, and let it cool our desires. Is it my very meat to do the will of Him that sent me to this hospital, to this room, to this bed, to this chair? If that work of endurance be not finished yet, do I want to escape it? No, Lord, no; never would I choose that choice of cowardice. When I feel as though I did, hold Thou me up and I shall be safe.

These letters, written in fragments, are posted home in my seventeenth month. But what are seventeen months? "It is seventeen years since I sat up," wrote one to me lately from a London hospital. And as once before I saw great matters through a small window, so through this little pane of glass I see the greater trials of many.

I wonder if they find as I do that even though their will has long ago been folded up in the blessed Will of God, a strangely persistent *I* can rise up suddenly, and in startling and unexpected fashion discover chaff upon the floor. It was in such an hour the song of this letter was born.

Is it not good to know that of His work in us on earth, even as of His work through us, there will come a day, when He will say, "It is finished," the chaff all winnowed, the *I* slain, never to take life again, the silver cleansed from the scum of earth, the soul perfect as a flower, and we shall be like Him then, for we shall see Him as He is?

And now? The heart that loves has only one answer to that: "He shall choose our interitance for us." I remember with what delight I found in Young's *Analytical Concordance* that the verb in this verse is the same as that used to show David choosing, out of all possible stones in the brook, the five best for his purpose. So does our heavenly David, our Beloved, choose out of all possible circumstances (and they are all at His command) the best for the fulfillment of His purpose. As I write these words a Tamil chorus, written for the battle of years ago, is being sung in the room near mine. A little band is setting forth for Hero's Town, a dark and very evil place where in a wonderful way a house has been given to us. Now the cheery bustle of the send-off comes up to me. Does the whisperer ever forget to come and whisper his appeal to that persistent *I:* "How good to be there again! When will that day come? How long it is in coming!" No, he never forgets, but I have found a certain and swift deliverance in turning on the instant to Him who is nearer than any whisperer: "Make pure my inmost heart's desire." And then comes peace, and with it assurance. However things may appear to be, of all possible circumstances, this in whose midst we are set is the best that He could choose. We do not know how that is true—where would faith be if we did?—but we do know that all things that happen are full of shining seed. Light is sown for us—not darkness.

One day, deep in the forest, we came upon a rock in midstream scooped by the backwash of immemorial waters to a hollow like the palm of a man's hand.

Over this rock fell a crystal sheet of water, and through that moving clearness we saw maidenhair fern growing in lovely profusion in the hollow of the hand. It was not the place where we should have planted a fern; at any moment it might have been tossed, a piteous, crumpled mass, down the shouting river—this is how it seemed to us. But it was safe. The falls flowed over it, not on it. And it was blessed. When the fern on the bank shriveled in heat, it was green, for it was watered all the year long by dust of spray. So does our wonderful God turn that which had seemed to be a perpetual threat to a perpetual benediction. Is there anything to fear with such a God?

There is another thought which, though it is often with me, I have not written yet. Today a St. Thomas' nurse who has read these letters (for I would not have courage to let them go if it were not that such a one has read them and wants them) brings that thought to mind, and sends me her own little copy of *The Sermon in the Hospital*, with the words marked which speak of the passion of regret that would surely overcome us if today our Lord should say "It is finished":

> Thou wouldst say, "So soon?
> Let me go back, and suffer yet awhile
> More patiently; I have not yet praised God."

So let us praise Him now, though it may be from under the harrow, from the depths, from anywhere. We shall never have the chance again to love Him in the peace of a great contentment, with the word ringing in our ear, "And blessed is he whosoever shall not be offended in Me."

The Beloved clothed Himself in the garment of His Lover, that he might be His companion in glory for ever. So the Lover desired to wear crimson garments daily, that his dress might be like that of his Beloved.

These words, more than six centuries old, from *The Book of the Lover and the Beloved,* have come to mean much to some of us.

ANOTHER SHALL GIRD THEE

ARE these the days when thou dost gird thyself
And walkest where thou wouldest, battle days,
Crowded and burdened and yet lit with praise,
Days of adventure; eager, glorious choice
Folded in every hour? Rejoice, rejoice,
   O happy warrior, if so it be,
   For surely thou shalt see
Jesus Himself draw near and walk with thee.

Or doth another gird thee, carry thee
Whither thou wouldest not, and doth a cord
Bind hand and foot, and flying thought and word?
An enemy hath done it, even so,
(Though why that power was his thou dost not know)
   O happy captive, fettered and yet free,
   Believe, believe to see
Jesus Himself draw near and walk with thee.

So either way is blessed; either way
Leadeth unto the Land of Heart's Desire;
Thy great Companion's love can never tire;
He is thy confidence, He is thy Song;
Let not thy heart be troubled, but be strong,
   O happy soul, to whom is given to see
   On all the roads that be,
Jesus Himself draw near and walk with thee.

35. WHITHER THOU WOULDEST NOT

THIS song came this morning in an hour so low that it would not rise even at the call of a book.

Beside me is a glass filled with wild begonia and young cinnamon from the forest; the flower-stem is crimson, the flower pinkish; the leaf-stem crimson, the polished leaf pale jade and the transparent pink of a shell or a cloud. I never before saw those two wild things together; they are unusual in loveliness. And as unusual but quick with a deeper beauty, never seen before by me, is the commingling of thought that I tried to capture in song, as I waited for a loosening of the cords that would set me free to do the things planned for the day.

Thou girdedst thyself, and walkedst whither thou wouldest. . . . Another shall gird thee, and carry thee whither thou wouldest not . . . . Jesus Himself drew near, and went with them.

For some of us life falls into two halves like that first sentence, which is double in content. Whither thou wouldest, whither thou wouldest not: service and suffering—and throughout both the Presence of the Risen Lord. For as He was with Peter, so He will be with us; He will not fail us nor forsake us.*

* *Forsaken* is in the Greek a compound of three words: "to leave behind

He drew near and went with each several disciple along the difficult road. They wore no halo then. They were human as we are. There is something that moves the heart in the story of the human Peter, over-persuaded by his friends, escaping from prison, hastening along the Appian Way, met by his Lord and Master—"Lord, whither goest Thou?" "I go to Rome to be crucified again for thee." And Peter turned back to his cell.

These letters are for the fettered (but the free) who are girded by another. They are being carried whither they would not. Who would go where they go now? But they do not go alone. Jesus Himself draws near and goes with them.

It is now evening. The sun set an hour ago behind the mountains; one by one the stars are dropping through the dim grey-blue, but an Indian robin, he who sang in starshine before sunrise this morning, and again in the hottest hour of noon when every other bird was still, is singing. This day of mine, so "lost," as it seems, but for that one little song this morning and these few words this evening, will not be lost if to one whom Pain is closely girding a thought of peace may come through that word of eternal consolation, *Jesus Himself drew near, and went with them.*

---

in." It conveys the idea of leaving comrades exposed to peril in the conflict, or forsaking them in some crisis of danger. *Fail* means to loose hold, so as to withdraw support of sustaining grasp. "I will in no wise desert you or leave you alone in the field of contest or in a position of suffering. I will in no wise let go my sustaining grasp." This word *fail* does not occur elsewhere in the New Testament in this sense.—See Westcott on Hebrews 13:5.

And where the road turns, Another waits (this time a friendly Another), to carry us whither we would be. "Carried by angels" is our Lord Jesus' way of telling us about that, and He knew. By such gentle hands He brings us unto our desired haven.

THE world is still. Sunset and moonlight, meeting,
 Lay long soft shadows on the dusty road;
The sheep are folded, not a lamb is bleating:
 Fold me, O God.

The feverish hours have cooled, and ceased the
  wrestling
 For place and power, fallen the last loud word;
Only a mother calls her wayward nestling,
 "Come, little bird."

Never a stir, but 'tis Thy hand that settles
 Tired flowers' affairs, and piles a starry heap
Of night-lights on the jasmine. Touch my petals:
 Put me to sleep.

It is God's will that we take His behests and His
comfortings as largely and as mightily as we may take
them, and also He willeth that we take our abiding
and our troubles as lightly as we may take them, and
set them at nought. For the more lightly we take
them, and the less price we set on them, for love, the
less pain we shall have in the feeling of them, and the
more thanks and meed we shall have for them.

JULIAN OF NORWICH.

36. BAD NIGHTS—FUNGI

Fastened across my foot-rest chair, where the bluebells used to be, is a branch of dead wood. On it is growing one of the peculiar treasures of our tropical forest, a fungus which opens like a saucer, sometimes so small that it looks like the saucer of a fairy cup, sometimes more than six inches across. The saucer is made of a kind of brittle satin. It has the sheen of satin. It may choose any shade of gold it likes, pale as rice in harvest, rich as wheat, or ruddy as the leaves of copper beech; but its decoration is always the same, ring after ring of its own color deepening to a lovely brown. It may please itself about its edge, curve it like a flower, flute it, or carry it round plain; but often it works out a delicate pattern there, like that of a moth's wing. There are eleven of these delights on the branch before me. On a bigger one, tied up behind the tigress' head above my bookcase, there are one hundred and fifteen. (She looks at home among these woodland things.)

I want to return to the matter of a previous letter, the temptations of some illnesses, for I think that many may be where I am now. When "something to give you a good night" has failed, and a long string of failures, or what your nurse calls "bad nights," lie behind, so that you begin to reach the end of your sanguine expectations—then is the time that mental mosquitoes, silly and small, can swarm about you, or something lizard-like crawls and darts. One, the worst of the tribe, changes color as you watch. Nothing is too fantastic for the chameleon.

In old days, when it was too hot to sleep, even under the stars, I used to make nonsense rhymes for the children, or sometimes songs. One of these, whose last line, "Touch my petals: Put me to sleep," has often recurred of late, belongs to a time when the Hindus who live near us were very vocal over something they thought important, and a shepherd with his noisy flock of mixed goats and sheep had established himself on the other side of what was then a low mud wall. But on the night of that song the Hindu village was asleep and so was the flock. Our household was asleep too, all lights were turned low except the lanterns of the night-loving flowers; I can still see the large white jasmine near my cane cot and smell its faint sweetness. There was no reason (except heat, which does not count) for lying awake, and yet sleep fled.

It can be so with the ill. There may be no good reason for sleeplessness; the clamors of acute pain have passed. How futile, then, is this way of spending time, a way that will make tomorrow so much harder, so much more ineffective. With that comes the high, thin note of the questing mosquito, teasing the ear. It is a long-drawn *Why?* Why does not the velvet curtain fall, whose soft folds fall so gently that we never know the moment when they wrap us round in peace? Why cannot we find the way into the land which is not a hand-breadth distant? And the changeful chameleon darts upon us from nowhere, as it seems; now this, now that trifle appears as a trial, made large by the magnifying lens of night, or dark before dawn, into something that fills all the air, and (this is why I think of this kind of temptation as chameleon-like in habit) what in a reasonable hour appears as a comfort, changes color and looks like a trouble. Mosquito or chameleon, they are disturbing creatures.

And then, like tired children, we turn to our Father:

It is Thy hand that settles
  Tired flowers' affairs, and piles a starry heap
Of night-lights on the jasmine. Touch my petals:
  Put me to sleep.

And still we do not sleep. Why?

I have found that in the end that prayer is answered, if not by sleep, then in something even better, the peace that passes all understanding, peace without explanation, peace that can take the edge off the morning's weariness and make the impossible possible. It is the old word turned to blessed fact, "When He giveth quietness, who then can make trouble?" So does He touch our petals, so does He cause His dews of quietness to fall upon His flowers, so does He bring out of the dead wood of a bad night a little thing for His praise.

YET listen now,
Oh, listen with the wondering olive trees,
And the white moon that looked between the leaves,
And gentle earth that shuddered as she felt
Great drops of blood. All torturing questions find
Answer beneath those old grey olive trees.
There, only there, we can take heart to hope
For all lost lambs—aye, even for ravening wolves.
Oh, there are things done in the world to-day
Would root up faith, but for Gethsemane.

For Calvary interprets human life;
   No path of pain but there we meet our Lord;
And all the strain, the terror and the strife
   Die down like waves before His peaceful word,
And nowhere but beside the awful Cross,
   And where the olives grow along the hill,
Can we accept the unexplained, the loss,
   The crushing agony, and hold us still.

37 THY CALVARY STILLS ALL OUR QUESTIONS

THIS that I write now is meant only for those who are harassed by the existence of pain. Children who love their Father know that when He says, "All things work together for good to them that love God," He must mean the best good, though how that can be they do not know. This is a *Why?* of a different order from that of the little mosquito. It is immeasurably greater. It strikes at the root of things. Why is pain at all, and *such* pain? Why did God ask Satan the question which (apparently) suggested to the Evil One to deal so cruelly with an innocent man? Why do the innocent so often suffer? Such questions generally choose a time when we are in keen physical or mental suffering, and may (the questioner hopes *will*) forget our comfort. They seize us like fierce living things and claw at our very souls.

Between us and a sense of the pain of the world there is usually a gate, a kind of sluice gate. In our unsuffering hours it may be shut fast. Thank God, it is shut fast for tens of millions. But let severe pain come, and it is as though the torture in us touched a secret spring, and that door opens suddenly, and straight upon us pour the lava floods of the woe of a creation that groans and travails together.

It is only the very ignorant, or those who do not see what they read, who can forget that almost all the pages of every true book of history, and of most true biographies, even of those which tell of a search after truth in one or other of the worlds of thought and action, are stained blood red; and if one thinks at all, the heart-racking thought will not be refused, it is not past; it is going on—"groaneth and travaileth in pain together until now."

O Lord, why? Why didst Thou make flesh like a field threaded all over with roads and lanes where burning feet continually do pass? Men, women, children, beasts, birds, and some of the water-creatures—why, knowing what was to be, didst Thou make them so? And the spirit of man, tuned like a delicate stringed instrument to the lightest touch, why, when it was to be smitten as by red-hot rods, didst Thou make it so? Why build the house of life with every door set open to the devouring flame? It is a poignant *Why?*

I have read many answers, but none satisfy me. One often given is our Lord's to St. Peter: "What I do thou knowest not now; but thou shalt know hereafter." And yet it is not an answer. He is speaking there of something which He Himself is doing; He is not doing this. He went about undoing it. "Ought not this woman whom Satan hath bound be loosed?" That was always His attitude to suffering, and so that blessed word is not an answer to this question, and was not meant to be.

There are many poetical answers; one of these

satisfied me for a time:

> Then answered the Lord to the cry of His world,
>   "Shall I take away pain,
> And with it the power of the soul to endure,
>   Made strong by the strain?
> Shall I take away pity that knits heart to heart?
>   And sacrifice high?
> Will ye lose all your heroes that lift from the fire
>   White brows to the sky?
> Shall I take away love that redeems with a price,
>   And smiles at its loss?
> Can ye spare from your lives that would climb unto
>   Mine,
>   The Christ on the Cross?"

But, though, indeed, we know that pain nobly borne strengthens the soul, knits hearts together, leads to unselfish sacrifice (and we could not spare from our lives the Christ on the Cross), yet when the raw nerve in our own flesh is touched, we know, with a knowledge that penetrates to a place which these words cannot reach, that our question is not answered. It is only pushed farther back, for why should *that* be the way of strength, and why need hearts be knit together by such sharp knitting needles, and who would not willingly choose relief rather than the pity of the pitiful?

No; beautiful words do not satisfy the soul that is confined in the cell whose very substance is pain. Nor have they any light to shed upon the suffering of the innocent. They are only words. They are not an answer.

What, then, is the answer? I do not know. I believe that it is one of the secret things of the Lord, which will not be opened to us till we see Him who endured the Cross, see the scars in His hands and feet and side, see Him, our Beloved, face to face. I believe that in that revelation of love, which is far past our understanding now, we shall "understand even as all along we have been understood."

And till then? What does a child do whose mother or father allows something to be done which it cannot understand? There is only one way of peace. It is the child's way. The loving child trusts.

I believe that we who know our God, and have proved Him good past telling, will find rest there. The faith of the child rests on the character it knows. So may ours; so shall ours. Our Father does not explain, nor does He assure us as we long to be assured. For example, there is no word that I can find in the Bible that tells us that the faithful horse, which man's cruelty has maimed, will be far more than caused to forget on some celestial meadow; the dog betrayed far more than reassured; or that the little anguished child will be gathered in its angel's arms and there far more than comforted. But we know our Father. We know His character. Somehow, somewhere, the wrong must be put right; *how* we do not know, only we know that, because He is what He is, anything else is inconceivable. For the word sent to the man whose soul was among lions and who was soon to be done to death, unsuccored, though the Lord of Daniel was so near, is fathomless: "And blessed is he whosoever shall not be offended in Me."

There is only one place where we can receive, not an answer to our question, but peace—that place is Calvary. An hour at the foot of the Cross steadies the soul as nothing else can. "O Christ beloved, Thy Calvary stills all our questions." Love that loves like *that* can be trusted about this.

WINTER

When my leaves fall wilt Thou encompass them?
  The gold of autumn flown, the bare branch brown,
The brittle twig and stem,
  The tired leaves dropping down,
Wilt Thou encompass that which men call dead?
  I see the rain, the coldly smothering snow,
My leaves dispirited,
  Lie very low.

So the heart questioneth, white Winter near;
  Till jocund as the glorious voice of Spring
Cometh His, "Do not fear,
  But sing, rejoice and sing,
For sheltered by the coverlet of snow
  Are secrets of delight, and there shall be
Uprising that shall show
  All that through Winter I prepared for thee."

38. A DOOR OPENED IN HEAVEN

BUT the last letter must be to the ill, and especially to you, friend, whom I feel as though I knew, you who may not look forward to health. A letter came lately from one in a hospital for incurable patients. The address went to our hearts. Some who appear to live in such places do not really live there, they only stay there. They live under the open sky. The winds of God blow round them. But for some there must often be a closing in of earthly walls as they look forward, not to autumn with its golden glow, but to winter, stark winter.

It was my nurse's thought that there should be something just for these, and so this morning I spent an hour in spirit with them, and a word came which I believe can console not only the single prod of the harrow-tooth (the passing illness), but the multiple pains of the whole harrow; this is the word: "He knoweth the way that I take. Thou knowest my downsitting and mine uprising. Thou compassest my path and my lying down."

Has the day to be spent in bed? or in chair? or partly in both? Think of the Lord our God our Father, being about our lying down. Does it not seem as though He were searching for a word to tell us how near He is? And if He be so near as that, what can we have to fear? Does the flesh quail as imagination, vivid as ever, looks on to what may be? But *Dominus illuminatio mea* must be true:

> When the will has forgotten the lifelong aim,
> And the mind can only disgrace its fame,
> And a man's uncertain of his own name,
> The power of the Lord shall fill this frame.

My first memory as a tiny child is this: after the nursery light had been turned low and I was quite alone, I used to smooth a little place on the sheet, and say aloud, but softly, to our Father, "Please come and sit with me." And that baby custom left something which recurs and is with me still. *Our God is a God at hand,* and "To Him who is everywhere, men come not by travelling but by loving." Is not this good for us who cannot travel?.

He who compasses our lying down today will compass our lying down tomorrow; our falling leaves will fall into His hand. "Thou hast made summer *and winter.*"

How, then, can winter hurt us? It is for help, not hurt, a gentle preparation for a divine surprise. There is a brightness that our eyes could not bear to look upon now; they are too dim and tired. There are harmonies too ravishing, raptures too enchanting for ear and heart today. Flowers of eternal wonder, snowdrops of God, are folded in the coverlet of snow. And He who compasses our lying down shall encompass our uprising, so shall we ever be with the Lord.

This is why the song called *Winter* passes swiftly from sadness to that uplifting expectation which is the joy of faith. Every line of that little song came, as it were, in a hospital ward, by a bedside. It is for whoso will find a seed of light in it. One thought more, small, but like the honey that drops its unexpected sweetness from the comb high in the forest tree, a honeydrop new to me.

I was thinking of the long road to the Land at a great distance, and of how very delightful the work of a doctor must be when he can tell one who had expected to have far to walk that the road may be quite short; and of how more than delighted such a traveler must be; and of those to whom this letter is chiefly written who, so far as they know, have no such delight very near, when I remembered which of the Twelve was chosen to lay down his life for his brethren, not in the martyrdom of a moment, but in a stretch of painful years. It was the disciple whom Jesus loved, he who leaned upon His breast. And I wondered if our Lord Jesus, looking through the windows of that upper chamber on the long road, knowing how footsore the traveler would be, perhaps how lonely too ("They are all gone into the world of light, and I alone sit ling'ring here"), drew him close to His heart that evening, said to him in a language that only the heart hears, "O man, greatly beloved, fear not: peace be unto thee; be strong, yea be strong."

But the enemy has a poisonous way of tampering with our sweetness. Is the patient in the incurable hospital (or elsewhere) laying down his life for his brethren? Possibly John the prisoner, chained, scourged, sentenced to toil in the mines of Patmos under the overseer's lash, had his cup embittered by this drop of gall. It is a favorite poison. But our Lord knows how to sweeten bitter cups.

In South India we have no snow; instead of snow we have great heat. During the hot weather, when the leaves of the lilies fade, you (if you are wise) do not water the plant; you must not persuade it to make green leaves then; its powers are being used otherwise. For then, in this hot, silent time, the miracle is wrought that multiplies your lily bulb. In cold lands instead of heat there is the silent snowtime; shall we not trust whether through the heat or under the snow?

The first song of comfort in this little Rose book was just for myself. But the Mary who bestowed much labor on me overheard a melody for it; we could not keep that music for ourselves, so new words were "taken" for others. With these words our letters end. They leave us where we want to be; our brier is still a brier of earth, but penetrated and pervaded by something that is not of earth, like the rosebush of our gardens with its small pink roses and its fragrant leaves.

This worshiping song has often been part of that daily act of adoration and remembrance which holds the soul in quietness very near the Cross. Whatever be our name or sign, such moments set apart are possible; for even though the symbols cannot always be, and outward stillness may be often only a dream of desire, the heart of the true lover can retire into its cell, that "cell where Jesus is the door, His love the only key," and there spiritually receive from the Beloved Himself the Bread and Wine invisible. But there is a sacred and intimate joy which all may taste who will, when a portion of the common food of the day is hallowed by that so present Presence, and as at a meal of long ago the water becomes wine, and we know Thee, O Lord, our Redeemer; we know Thee in the breaking of bread; we meet Thee at the foot of the Cross; we meet Thee in the Garden in the sunrise.

Have we not seen Thy shining garment's hem
Floating at dawn across the golden skies,
Through thin blue veils at noon, bright majesties,
Seen starry hosts delight to gem
The splendour that shall be Thy diadem?

O Immanence, that knows nor far nor near,
But as the air we breathe is with us here,
Our Breath of Life, O Lord, we worship Thee.

Worship and laud and praise Thee evermore,
Look up in wonder, and behold a door
Opened in heaven, and One set on a throne;
Stretch out a hand, and touch Thine own,
O Christ, our King, our Lord whom we adore.

INDEX OF SONGS FACING LETTERS

THE DOHNAVUR FELLOWSHIP

The work in Dohnavur still continues, but now the Fellowship members are all of Indian nationality. They do not belong officially to any of the organized churches; but in fellowship with others of God's children, they seek to make His love and salvation known to all whom they can reach.

The dedication of girls to the temples is now illegal, but the Fellowship provides a home for children who might otherwise fall into the hands of people who would exploit them in some way.

Girls of all ages from babies to teenagers form a large part of the family in Dohnavur. The need to care for them continues until they are securely launched elsewhere or else have become fellow workers. The aim is still to bring them up to know and love our Lord Jesus and to follow His example as those who desire not to be served but to serve others.

The hospital treats patients from the surrounding countryside. They are from varied religious backgrounds—Hindu, Muslim, Christian. They include rich and poor, highly educated and illiterate. Through this medical work God continues to bring to us the people we long to reach, those whose need is for spiritual as well as physical healing.

Boys are no longer admitted, but the buildings they occupied are now put to full use. In 1981 the Fellowship in partnership with other Christians formed the Santhosha Educational Society to administer a co-educational English-medium boarding school, primarily for the benefit of the children of missionaries of Indian nationality. The buildings provide facilities for over 300 children now studying there. Their parents come from Indian missions and organizations working in many parts of India, including tribal areas.

In matters of finance, we follow the pattern shown from the beginning of the work. Amy Carmichael rejoiced in her Heavenly Father's faithfulness in supplying each need. We praise Him that His faithfulness is the same today.

The Dohnavur Fellowship
Tirunelveli District
Tamil Nadu 627 102
India

The Dohnavur Fellowship
15 Elm Drive
North Harrow
Middlesex HA2 7BS
England